A search for self

Making a *friend* out of the *stranger* within

Thirtysix.org

A Search for Self

Making a Friend out of the Stranger Within

ISBN 9781731528476

Published by:
Thirtysix.org
22 Yitzchak Road
Telzstone, Kiryat Yearim
Israel   90838

Dedicated

contents

introduction

THERE IS A lot of knowledge out there, but little of it gives us as much pleasure as the kind that helps us better understand ourselves. Life is filled with many strangers, including people we pass in the street, most of whom we NEVER get to know or understand. We barely get to do that with people we associate with on a regular basis. But why live with someone we CAN know and understand but don't?

SELF-knowledge[1] is where it's at. The more you know about yourself, who you are and what you are capable of being like, the less surprised

---

[1] This will be the topic of Chapter 1.

you will be when you find out more. It's better to make a friend out of the stranger inside you than to find out that the companion inside you is really a stranger. Some people never quite recover from THAT.

Perhaps it wouldn't be so necessary if the world were just far more mundane.[2] Then life would be the same every single day, and it would have no surprises. You could be sure that what you see today will be the same thing you will see every day henceforth, and that the people you know will always be the same. Then YOU could always be the same as well.

As hard as some people have tried to make their life work out that way, they were not successful. Life is just not like that. The WORLD is not like that. The world is infinitely diverse. It changes people in ways they could never predict. And if we do not get with THAT program, then we're going to have a VERY difficult time fitting in, being "normal," and achieving happiness.

Psychiatry is a VERY busy field, and the pharmaceutical industry makes BIG bucks. Self-help books take a huge chunk of the book market. In most cases people buy these books AFTER the problem has occurred, after the "stranger within"

---

[2] This is the subject of Chapter 2.

has made a surprise appearance. Then often with much anguish, and by using up very valuable resources, they become acquainted with other parts of their personality.

Today it's even harder to know oneself than ever before. Modern man, in his wisdom,[3] thought that by ridding himself of religion, he was in fact increasing his freedom. Surprise, surprise: he has never been more enslaved.

Once upon a time, people grew up with the belief that there were certain facets to their personality, and not all of them were good. They believed in things like demons and angels, beings that today we look at only as creations of religious imagination.[4] And they believed in the evil inclination, a.k.a. the yetzer hara, which began as a snake in Paradise, but which was absorbed after THE sin into the inner being of everyone.

Granted, the early understanding of this negative dynamic of being human was often unsophisticated and even abused, especially by religious leaders. But when their "other" side appeared, they could make something of it, and often fight it against it. True, it was often complicated and made life difficult, but who says that is

---

[3] This is the subject of Chapter 3.
[4] This is the subject of Chapter 4.

necessarily a BAD thing?

The modern world does. It knows that pain is an intrinsic part of life, and that struggle is usually part and parcel of success. But it also believes that it should be possible to control when and where struggle and pain should occur, and it spends a lot of time and energy on this. As far as the modern world is concerned, we're here to enjoy ourselves, and that means minimizing the struggles in life.

Therefore bye, bye yetzer hara. It's just extra intellectual baggage, unnecessarily making people feel bad for things they think, say, or do. Humans have problems. They don't have perfect childhoods. Life can be confusing and tough. The human mind is very complex. The art of life is trying to live within the communally accepted framework, minimizing the damage you do to yourself and to others. Society doesn't ask you to be great, just not to be too "bad."

So how's that working out for society?

It depends on where you're standing. If you're in the thick of it, you can be so swept up in the momentum that you can't even see how crazy the world has become, and how much you have become a part of the insanity. All the evil reported in the newspapers is treated like "another day at the office." Tragedy.

If we take a few steps back, we will notice that something is not right, and perhaps, from time to time, even complain about the way things are. But that's about as far as we go, other than perhaps turning off the news early because we can't stand to listen to what is going on in the world of which we are still very much a part.

However, those who step back far enough,[5] far enough to see the world more as God does, clearly know that something is VERY wrong. There are still a lot of "good" people in the world today, but overall the world seems to have lost its way. Today still becomes tomorrow, and on into decades and centuries. But as the world nears the end of its SIXTH millennium, where is it really heading? How much does mankind understand itself?

A philosopher once stated, "I think, therefore I am." Many people believe that just because they THINK, they ARE. Are WHAT? The best they are MEANT to be? As happy as they CAN be? As moral as they SHOULD be? There is a spiritual passageway between two very different levels of living which belong to each and every one of us. We only need to "think" to access the first level. We need SELF-KNOWLEDGE to access the second

---

[5] This is the subject of Chapter 5.

one. It is the key.

    There IS a lot of knowledge out there. But so much is only a distraction away from the knowledge that counts the most: knowledge of self.

THIS SHOULD BE a very short chapter. After all, how much can you write about self-knowledge? As the name states explicitly, it is knowledge about your self. You don't even need to go online to find out about that one.

Hah! It should only be so easy. There are plenty of books out there teaching about self-knowledge, and most of them have LOTS of pages. Staring at yourself in the mirror apparently doesn't increase your self-knowledge all that much, at least not enough to enhance your life significantly.

People have spent tens of thousands of dollars, travelled halfway across the world, and have even cut themselves off from society, all in search of knowledge of their self. The question is whether or not they were successful in the end.

A good starting point is figuring out exactly what we mean when we refer to "self." Although it's such a short little word, it hides in plain sight one of the biggest questions of life: What IS the self?

Most people have no idea what their self is because they spend so much time looking outward rather than inward. Although we have little control over the world around us, we must still navigate through life from day to day. There's plenty out there to keep us preoccupied for our entire life and, for most, it usually does.

Sometimes, however, we're forced to take a break from the outside world and look inside. Crises will do that. They make us act in ways we don't recognize and feel things we have never felt before. Suddenly, a part of us that has never before spoken up takes control, making some people wonder if they have a kind of personality disorder.

This can shake us to our core. Depending on a number of factors, we may (1) simply move on or (2) spend time finding out more about our "mysterious" self. The first approach, just moving on, is a band-aid solution, and may have negative consequences down the line if a personality crisis occurs. The second approach results in far greater self-awareness and self-control, and THAT leads to greater accomplishments in life.

One person, for example, took a year off from life. He didn't travel east, west, north, or south. Instead he travelled back in time, deciding to "rebuild" his memory, year by year, to the best of his ability. It barely cost him anything at all, but the rewards were immense.

The first thing he did was to gather together old pictures of himself, as many as he could find, going as far back as possible. He put them into an album, according to age, to remind himself of what he was like as a baby, an adolescent, and then as a teenager. At present he looks much older than in all the pictures, but all of "them" are still inside him.

When he looked at the pictures, he would try to recall what the world seemed like to him at the time each picture was taken. It was difficult, usually impossible, but sometimes insightful. It is amazing how many memories come back to our CONSCIOUS mind when we work hard to remember them. They're always there of course, stored away in the UNCONSCIOUS mind and somehow contributing to the reality of the person at any given age, but they're rarely accessed.

Next, he "interviewed" as many people who

knew him in his early years as he could find. He wanted to know what they remembered most about him, what struck them as being special about him. He was piecing together a personality puzzle, and although he could not get ALL the pieces, whatever he could find was a lot more than he had known previously.

With each new detail about his former years, he felt as if he were getting to know himself much better. A year later he was already a different person—well, actually the same person, but more of that person. The experience had changed him, and everything he learned about himself seemed to have a place to fit inside him.

This was because, in truth, there wasn't anything anyone could tell him about himself that he didn't already know, on some level. What people had in fact done was to help bring his hidden self-knowledge to his conscious mind, where he could identify it and work with it.

Today this person knows himself far better than most people know themselves. He is stronger for it, and able to more meaningfully direct himself through life.

From this it would seem as if self is an accumulated reality, an ongoing result of all the external realties that have interacted with our internal being. Yes, we come into this world with certain "givens," but life seems to be a matter of how those "givens" interact with the world around us.

But is that really what the self is? Aren't our life experiences just a way to "force" our self, whatever it is, out into the open? We're born with something that is uniquely us, but what IS it?

A soul.

A SOUL?

YES, a soul.[1]

Many people who believe that they have a soul view it merely as a spiritual "component." They don't see it as the self itself, but rather as a spiritual entity whose job is to bring some sense of conscience to the personality table. They don't understand that it is the sum total of all a person is capable of becoming.

That is not to say that the body with which we are born has nothing to say about who we are and what we do in life.

Consider a car. All the "bells and whistles" can enhance a car's driving performance only so much. On the other hand, a car needs moving parts to actualize the engine's potential, and the higher the quality of the materials and the engineering, the more the engine is able to do what it

---

1 Sha'ar HaGilgulim, Introduction 1.

needs to.

Likewise, the soul NEEDS the body to fulfill itself. In fact it is quite dependent upon the body it is in, and therefore limited by it in accomplishing anything. The soul may dream of scaling great heights, but will have a difficult time doing so if the body doesn't want to get out of bed each morning.

The bottom line is that SELF-knowledge is SOUL-knowledge. To know your SELF is to know your SOUL. To try to understand the self merely by how it functions in the body is like trying to understand an engine by the way the car drives. You can learn something, but how accurate can the information be if it is only a combination of what the engine AND body are, and how they work together?

But look under the hood...

THE SOUL IS a spark of Divine Light. It can do no wrong. All a soul wants to do is connect to God and live a purely spiritual existence.[1] That will become very obvious in the Messianic Era, when everyone alive will do only that, even while still in their body.

However, identifying the self as the soul seemingly does little to further the cause of self-knowledge. After all, how can we know anything about our soul? Because it's invisible, some people have come to believe that they don't even have one. How then can we learn anything about it?

---

[1] Niddah 30b.

By the way we drive.

Not our car, but our life.

Marketing studies sometimes ask children under the age of 13 for their opinions. Around 13, a person becomes a "Bar Da'as,"[2] and begins to consider what a questioner wants to hear. Until then, children are still innocent enough to speak their own minds, without second-guessing themselves. This idea can be used with respect to soul-knowledge as well.

Even though the soul is of no particular age, it has a childlike innocence. It is honest and not calculating, pure and unadulterated. Although "man" is capable of unspeakable evils, none of them come from the soul, as will be discussed in the next chapter. Ask the soul a question, and you get ITS answer.

It's like a knee-jerk reaction, because it is automatic and unthinking, a reflex answer. Because of this, souls are usually considered careless, irresponsible, and even potentially dangerous. That is why the first mishnah in Pirkei Avos advises us to be deliberate in judgment.[3]

---

2 Literally, "Son of Knowledge," a term used to describe an age of intellectual maturity at which a person becomes halachically responsible for his or her actions.

3 Pirkei Avos 1:1.

This is excellent advice for making decisions. But sometimes people say things to us that we did not expect, and events can seem to happen "out of nowhere." Caught off guard, our brain goes into reaction mode, before we even have a chance to deliberate.

But it is exactly these raw responses to life's situations that are the most instructive about who we really are. Whatever we become in life, even for the most deliberate and thoughtful people, we are still only able to work with our givens and with the soul that we have—or rather are.

A soul has an innate nature. It is prone to certain tendencies, which nurturing serves to either bring out or suppress. Like a bumper car, we get knocked around throughout life and sent off in one direction or another. How we survive those bumps and jolts depends on several factors, the main one being the type of soul we have.

Kabbalah defines different soul natures in significant detail.[4] For all intents and purposes, we see them in everyday life, and we can see that basically there are pairs. Depending upon which soul-nature we have, we will either be short-tempered or patient, vengeful or forgiving, more inter-

---

[4] See my book "Reincarnation Again" for some of these soul details.

ested in receiving love or giving it, strict or laid back, highly disciplined, loosely organized, etc.

The interesting thing is that, no matter what the soul nature is, EVERYONE wants the same thing in life: SELF-FULFILLMENT. We all wants to become the very best person we can possibly become, because it is the only thing that makes us feel that life is worthwhile. This is a soul thing, and therefore innate to our existence.

To succeed in this goal, we have also been given intelligence. It's what allows us to learn about ourselves, so that we can adapt our circumstances and attitudes to maximize our success in life. In fact, we do this quite naturally just to survive and get ahead in life.

The only problem is that what society wants from us and what we ULTIMATELY want from ourselves can be very different. Consequently, we can end up using our intelligence and ability to adapt and grow in the wrong areas, wasting precious time and ability that are necessary to accomplish the true goal in life.

It would be brilliant if parents and teachers recorded children's tendencies in their early stages for future reference. They would be compiling valuable soul-knowledge that grown-up children could later use to better understand how and why they got to where they were.

It would be even better if parents and educators shared that knowledge with their children as they were growing up, so that it could become part of their consciousness as they grew older. We also need programs to help children learn how to adapt their innate nature to the world around them in order to maximize their efficiency in life, rather than their getting the same knowledge haphazardly, if at all.

This is what we need to do: we need to write a diary about our life, past, present, and future. We want to record not only what has happened to us, but how we dealt with it. We need to figure out what it means about our soul-nature, and then how to use the insights to our advantage in the future.

For example, one person always imagined himself as being a calm and collected person, but he usually got uptight when something upset his balance. Later on, after he was married with children, he would often come home from work in a great mood, feeling he had accomplished a lot during his day, and being happy about it.

He would walk through the front door in that mood, and invariably watch it crumble within minutes. Between dealing with the children, housework, and getting supper ready, his wife was at her wit's end. He came home at "cruising speed," but she came at him from the opposite direction like a train out of control.

It usually didn't take long for him to feel resentment for having been forced to leave his good mood at the door. The interchange that followed often became hostile, making the situation only worse. His wife might eventually walk away angry and feeling under-appreciated, and he would feel robbed of his hard-earned peace of mind.

When this scenario kept repeating itself, he finally wised up. He had to go home. He had to walk through the front door. His family situation was what it was. The only variable in the equation, he realized, was he himself. HE was the one who was aware of what kept happening, and HE definitely wanted to avoid it.

He gave it some serious thought. The more he did, the more he realized that as much as he had THOUGHT he was a naturally calm person, he was really more a person who loved being calm. In the past he had maintained the appearance of being calm by avoiding confrontational situations. When he could not avoid them, he recalled that he had had a difficult time remaining even remotely calm.

It was an obvious oversight, now that he paid attention to it. His family situation brought it to light, and it made him look back on his life to see the earlier signs that indicated that he did not have a naturally calm demeanor.

To make a long story appropriately short, his updated vision of his essential nature was able to reveal to him why certain aspects of life, like being organized and disciplined, came easily to him, whereas not feeling jealous over the success of others didn't. He had to work at things like that.

In the meantime, his front door stopped being a portal to crisis. He figured out a way to work around the situation, without sneaking in through the backdoor. Instead, he praised his wife's efforts when he first walked in, and made a point of making the children laugh or at least smile when he saw them. Over time everyone's mood lightened up, and his experience when coming home was completely transformed.

This wasn't the only good news. The soul insight spilled over into other areas of his life as well, affecting the choices he made, how he interacted with other people, and how he dealt with crises. His life wasn't perfect but it is was certainly a LOT better, as were the lives of the people around him.

We could discuss the kabbalistic understanding of soul natures and, for many, it could be helpful. But it's not really all that necessary, not here at least. Just by being observant and perceptive about our most natural tendencies and reactions in life, we can reverse-engineer the kabbalistic definitions. The words may vary, but the understanding will be the same.

WHAT GOES wrong? How can a self that's a soul that only wants to do good be responsible for so much bad? How can something that longs to be close to God do so much to distance itself from Him?

It's really not the soul's fault. To explain why, some background information is necessary, some KABBALISTIC information.

Once upon a time, there was only one man in the world, Adam "the First," or Adam HaRishon in Hebrew. Although this first man WAS human, he was not at all like we are today. Not only was he a giant of a person,[1] physically and spiritually, he didn't even look at all like us. He had all the same body parts, but they were more spiritual than physical.[2] His skin was more light than skin, and if that first man were to stand before us today, we probably would not even be able to see him.

Did the first man have a soul? Did he EVER! In fact, when Adam HaRishon was first created, his soul was a composite of ALL souls that would ever come into the world from the time he was created until the Messianic Era, which, the last time we checked, had not yet officially started.[3] Adam was not only the first of mankind, he WAS mankind.

Then he sinned. God had told Adam, who by that time had a wife, Chava, not to eat from the Aitz HaDa'as Tov v'Ra, the now infamous Tree of Knowledge of Good and Evil.[4] But as the Torah reports, they defied Him and ate anyhow. As Kabbalah explains, by so doing they transformed themselves and the entire universe.[5]

That's when Adam, Chava, and their five

---

[1] Chagigah 12a.

[2] Drushei Olam HaTohu, Drush Aitz HaDa'as, Siman 4.

[3] Sha'ar HaGilgulim, Introduction 29.

[4] Bereishis 3:6.

[5] Drushei Olam HaTohu, Drush Aitz HaDa'as, Siman 4; Hakdamos u'Sha'arim, Sha'ar 6, Ch. 10-11.

children[6] became more like us. They became more physical, their skin of light turning into actual flesh, and their physiques becoming more "normal," necessitating death and therefore expulsion from Paradise.

The most dramatic change to Adam HaRishon was to his soul. It no longer incorporated all souls, but only his own.[7] All the other souls "fell" from his soul. This not only left his soul greatly decreased, but also ours, diminishing our spiritual capability. Becoming more physical also meant that Adam was bound by physical limitations he previously had not known. History as we know it had begun.

What about all the rest of the souls? If they fell, where did they fall to?

To the klipos.[8] All of them fell into the klipos. What are the klipos? THAT is a long and involved kabbalistic discussion, but the long and short of it is that the klipos are the spiritual source of evil in the world—as they were created to be. By nature, they exist to interfere with a person's relationship with God, primarily through spiritual desensitization because that leads to sin and heresy.

---

[6] Kayin, Hevel, and their twin sisters (Bereishis Rabbah 22:2-3).
[7] Sha'ar HaGilgulim, Introduction 29.
[8] Sha'ar HaGilgulim, Introduction 29.

Hence their name "klipos," which means "peels," because like a peel, they intercede between what is on the inside—the soul—and on the "outside"—God. Unlike normal peels, they do it to protect themselves, not the person they have spiritually entrapped. Moshiach will come only after the klipos are gone from Creation.[9]

Falling into the klipos was very bad news, similar to stumbling into the most dangerous neighborhood in the universe with money hanging from your pockets, and wearing expensive clothing and jewelry. It will be highly unlikely that such an unfortunate soul will be able to just turn around and go out the way it came in.

The klipos "dine" on Divine Light, which is what souls are and what they generate. Klipos need it to survive and grow stronger so that they can take over the world and make it more like them.[10] They're always looking for more kedushah—holiness—to latch onto, and letting all Adam's souls fall into the klipos was similar to throwing live bait into a cage of ravenous lions.

The good news is that there is a way out. It's not an easy and quick process, but it works.[11]

---

[9] Sha'ar HaGilgulim, Introduction 20.
[10] Sha'ar HaGilgulim, Introduction 20.
[11] Sha'ar HaGilgulim, Introduction 12.

However, it also comes at a cost. Although we can take the soul out of the klipos, we cannot completely take the klipah out of the soul. Consequently, every soul that leaves the klipos does so with a personal klipah that clings to the soul like clothing to a body.[12] It's called the yetzer hara, or "evil inclination."

It's like being chained at the ankle to a criminal. When we pull him in our direction, he pulls us in his own. Being far more devious and selfish than us, he will strategize how best to overcome us.[13] He takes advantage of OUR nature to HIS ends, our ignorance to his benefit.

The klipah is the corrupting influence in a person's life. It has its own nature, and the more powerful a soul is, the more powerful the klipah's pull will be on the person. As Shlomo HaMelech wrote, "God has made one corresponding to the other,"[14] which means that for everything good there is a corresponding bad.

Once upon a time, it was easier to identify the klipos. They were external to man, appearing to him, at first, as the snake. They weren't any less tricky, as we see from the Torah, but at least Chava

---

12 Sha'ar HaGilgulim, Introduction 26.
13 Kiddushin 30b.
14 Koheles 7:14.

knew that the temptation to eat did not emanate from within her. Now it would, as it does within all of us, which is why it can so easily be mistaken for our own will.

The klipah is our Achilles heel. It is the "spy" living within us that opens the door to the enemy, making us vulnerable. When Rivkah, pregnant with Ya'akov and Eisav walked by a Bais Midrash, Ya'akov was drawn to it. When she walked by a place of idol worship, Eisav wanted to approach it. It's the same for us, our Ya'akov being the will of the soul, and our Eisav being our klipah.

It would be a mistake, however, to assume that the klipah is just a spiritual handicap that we have to adjust to while going about our life. It is rather the challenge of our life, something we're here to understand and eventually channel, as we learn after death.

This is the "$64,000 question" that we are asked after passing from this world: "What is the 'name' of your klipah?"[15] What happens to a person after the answer to that, either harsh Gehinom or the eternal bliss of the World-to-Come, depends upon the soul's ability to answer the question.

The name of our klipah is something we can

---

[15] Sha'ar HaGilgulim, Introduction 23.

only know well by taking the time to take note of our own spiritual weaknesses. By the time we die, we have to know which sins talked most to us, which mitzvos were the hardest to do. It wasn't our soul that made us commit that sin, or avoid that mitzvah. It was our klipah, and the sooner we are able to recognize it, the sooner we can stand up to its challenges.

This is not something that many people know about when they are growing up, or even after they have become adults. How many parents look at their children from this angle, intensely interested in understanding the soul nature of their child, and its klipah? Mostly you just hear, "He's a good boy;" "She's a talented young lady;" "He doesn't play well with other children;" "He doesn't pay enough attention to the teacher."

In other words, we look at our children as packages. They are what they are. They will be what they will be. We try to steer them properly whenever we can, but our judgment is based upon what we see at the time, without much thought given to what is really going on inside them. We end up either under- or over-compensating, adding more confusion to existing confusion.

It is remarkable how much we take ourselves and others for granted, how superficially we seem to deal with everyone. We see and relate to bodies.

We assume that what we think we see in the nature of others is their real self, and we are surprised when they respond to us in ways we may not understand.

Most people, when asked in the grave about the name of their klipah will probably answer, "What's a klipah?" It's one of those strange ironies of life where something is SO very important and yet SO neglected—SO central and yet SO ignored. And then we wonder why the world gets so crazy and so few people around can fix it.

But this wasn't Ya'akov Avinu's problem. His name may have been "heel,"[16] but not "Achilles Heel." No, Ya'akov was "Ish Emes," the "Man of Truth."[17] This means that even though he too had a personal klipah, like the rest of us, he knew what it was and how to deal with it. He never mistook it for himself, which is why he was able to say three words that most of us never can, at least not with the same level of sincerity.

But that is the topic of the next chapter.

---

[16] The root letters of "Ya'akov" are Ayin-Kuf-Bais, which spells "heel," since Ya'akov latched onto Eisav's heel at birth. (Bereishis 25:24).

[17] Michah 7:20; Makkos 24a.

chapter four: ish emes

ONE OF THE most amusing aspects of Torah is how the stories it tells can seem to be the opposite of the morals being taught. Nowhere is this more the case than with Ya'akov Avinu—Ish Emes, the Man of Truth.

Ya'akov may have started off as Ish Emes, but everything changed on the day that Eisav came home famished, and Ya'akov used the opportunity to compel Eisav to sell his birthright.[1] Decades later, when it came time for Eisav to receive his blessing from his father, Ya'akov disguised himself as Eisav, at his mother's insistence,

____

[1] Bereishis 25:29.

to receive the blessing instead.

How untruthful can you get?

The story doesn't end there either. There were other "tricks" that Ya'akov used during his journey to becoming the father of the Jewish people that others, like his father-in-law Lavan, would call into question. Even the Torah called it "stealing" when Ya'akov "stole" away with all his family and belongings while Lavan was off on a business trip.[2] And this was the "Man of Truth"?

The answer is obvious from everyday life. Truth is ABSOLUTE, but fulfilling it can depend upon circumstances. For example, the Talmud says that a person can "change the truth" for the sake of "shalom bayis," peace in the home.[3] Does this mean that spouses or children can lie just to selfishly save their own neck, as their klipah would have them do? No, not at all. It means that people can change the truth if doing so achieves a GREATER GOOD, one that the TORAH sanctions, as the soul would want them to do.

The key phrase here is "greater good." By definition, it MUST be in agreement with Torah, because we can only know what "good" really is through Torah, which is what Ya'akov Avinu em-

---

[2] Bereishis 31:20.
[3] Bava Metzia 87a.

bodied.[4] He was the level of Torah truth, GOD'S truth, and he saw the world and all of life in terms of it.

The rest of us learn and live Torah through our klipos. Torah gets distorted on the way in, and then we distort it further through performance of mitzvos. That is because we tend to serve God the way WE want to, not necessarily the way God wants us to serve Him.

This is why the Torah says:

Now, Israel, what does God, your God, ask of you? Only to fear God, your God... (Devarim 10:12)

Really? That's it? Just FEAR Him? What about the other 612 mitzvos mentioned in the Torah? Didn't He ask us to do THOSE too?

Of course. But to do those properly, a person has to fear God. It's the basis of SELF-HONESTY, or more accurately SOUL-honesty, because it has the power to mute the klipos. In a phrase, fear of God is humbling, and this allows a person to act like a soul and not like his klipah when learning Torah and living it.

This is why mitzvos will no longer be consid-

---

[4] Zohar, Vayishlach 170b.

ered mitzvos in Yemos HaMoshiach—the Messianic Era.[5] Mitzvos are eternal, so we'll ALWAYS do them in some way. But in Yemos HaMoshiach, once the yetzer hara is eliminated,[6] we will do them "naturally." As a soul in complete command of our body, we will jump out of bed in the morning to perform mitzvos, and return to bed at night only because we have no more strength left to do more mitzvos that day.

Thus, the Messianic Era is described as follows:

> God will be King over the entire land. On that day God will be One, and His Name, One. (Zechariah 14:9)

The only reason this is not true now is because of the klipos. They have the uncanny ability to distort reality and convince us that our perception of that reality is accurate, when in fact we are acting as if God is NOT King over the entire land.

They could not do this to Ya'akov Avinu. He WALKED the same earth as everyone else of his time, and interacted with them. But his con-

---

[5] Shabbos 151b; Avodah Zarah 3a; Drushei Olam HaTohu, Chelek 2, Drush 4, Anaf 12, Simanim 9-12.
[6] Succah 52a.

sciousness was messianic, meaning that he always thought of the endgame and acted accordingly. His body was just a means to get around and impact the world.

That is why, prior to his confrontation with Eisav his brother, he fought with the angel of Eisav. As the Midrash explains, the struggle is understood on many different levels, one of which is that Ya'akov actually fought with his own yetzer hara and prevailed. As a result, his name was changed to "Yisroel":

> Your name shall no longer be called Ya'akov, but Yisroel, because you have fought with [an angel of] God and with men, and you have prevailed. (Bereishis 32:28)

The "angel" was the Sitra Achra, a.k.a., the Satan, the angel of Eisav. The "men" were Lavan and Eisav, incarnations of the yetzer hara. Ya'akov fought and defeated them all, and that is what it means to be a TRUE "Yisroel," to live as a soul, not a klipah.

The net result of Ya'akov's victory and spiritual transformation was evident the next day, during his confrontation with Eisav. After Ya'akov tried to give his brother a gift, Eisav bragged that he already had a tremendous amount of possessions[7] and didn't need the gift.

Ya'akov was unimpressed, however. He really couldn't relate to having more material possessions than he needed in order to do what he was put on this earth to accomplish. Therefore, rather than brag to Eisav about all that he had, Ya'akov instead told Eisav, "Yaish lee kol, three words to express that he had all that he NEEDED. How many of us can say that? Ya'akov was happy with his portion, whatever it might be.

This is possible because the soul looks at the gift of life as exactly that, a gift. Every breath is a gift. Every part of the body is a gift. Whatever we have, from the soul's perspective, is more than we deserve. EVERY thing we get to use and enjoy, from a soul viewpoint, is always "icing on the cake," no matter what someone else has. A soul is here to do its job of rectifying itself. Why get bogged down, it asks of the klipah, in trappings of this world?

The klipah has its answer: What ELSE is there to do? Although the soul really starts to live only when the Messianic Era begins, that is when the klipos die. Therefore, any living the klipos CAN do is now, before Moshiach comes and rectifies the world, eliminating them forever.

---

[7] Bereishis 33:9.

That's the battle. The klipah wants to live for today only. The soul is only interested in living for the World-to-Come. Any pleasure it derives from this world is incidental, a wonderful by-product of living in this physical world. Material pleasure is certainly not a priority for the soul, as it is for the klipos.

But not for Ya'akov Avinu, whom the Talmud says never actually died.[8] How could he die? The klipos can "die," but the soul is ETERNAL. Since Ya'akov Avinu did not view himself as merely a soul "embedded" in a physical body, but as the soul itself, he was eternal his entire life. What Yosef embalmed was just the "casing" that housed the holy and great soul of his father.[9]

There's a story in the Talmud that makes the same point. A certain rabbi was seen by his students going somewhere, and they asked him where. He told them that he was going to honor his host, which made them even more curious, so they followed him.

To their surprise, their rabbi entered a bathhouse! When he later emerged, they asked him what he had meant because of where he had gone. He explained to them that his "host" was his

----

[8] Ta'anis 5b.
[9] Bereishis 50:2.

body, where his soul was a "guest." In appreciation, he treated his body to a bath, and took care of it.

This was the essential point of disagreement between the Hellenists and the Jews, which eventually led to the story of Chanukah. The Greeks identified with the physical aspect of man, beautifying and putting it on a pedestal. The Jewish people believed just the opposite, and fought with their lives to preserve the world of the soul.

The result was a victory over the Greeks against all odds, a miracle of finding one jar of ritually pure olive oil, and one day's worth of oil which supernaturally burned for seven extra days. It was enough for the rabbis to see fit to establish a unique holiday to celebrate the miracles, and they called the holiday "Chanukah."

Chanukah means "dedication," referring to what the Jewish people did with their newfound control over the Temple grounds. They rushed in and repaired what they could, rededicating the Temple, rekindling the Menorah with whatever oil they could find.

On a deeper level, the root of the word "Chanukah" is the word "chayn." It has been superficially translated as "grace," but as we learn from the story of Noach and later,[10] Yosef HaTzad-

---

[10] Bereishis 6:9.

dik,[11] it means so much more. It is a soul word, created when the soul is allowed to project itself to the outside world, like shemen zayis—olive oil—itself.

Shemen zayis—olive oil—has a lot in common with the soul. Both are hidden inside something solid and opaque, and both require a way to extract them before they can bring light to the darkness.

For the oil, the means of extraction is an olive press. For the soul, it is any deed that goes against the nature of the klipah. This sets up a confrontation between the soul and the yetzer hara, a fight to the finish. If the klipah prevails, the soil remains buried within and darkness results. If the soul prevails, as Ya'akov did over the angel of Eisav, the soul is "exposed" and light bursts forth into the world.

This was the battle between the "Peirushim"[12] and the "Misyavim,"[13] a battle between the Jewish soul and the klipos. The Greeks glorified the body and PHYSICAL accomplishments, the symbol of which was the olive. The Jews favored SPIRITUAL

---

[11] Rashi, Bereishis 49:22.

[12] "Separate" because they remained apart from the Secularists.

[13] The Hellenists.

greatness, symbolized by the oil hidden WITHIN the olive.

Hence, although the world looks at Greek culture as the source of light, just the opposite is true from a Torah perspective. As the Midrash says, the Greeks represent darkness,[14] which is why it was THEIR defeat that led to a holiday of light.

It is no simple matter to reach the level of an "Ish Emes." But we were given the Torah to help us try and, as the Talmud says, if we take small steps in the right direction, then Heaven will help us to succeed beyond our personal capability.[15] The starting point is learning to identify ourself as a soul, rather than the host to which it has been assigned.

---

[14] Bereishis Rabbah 2:4.
[15] Yoma 38b.

chapter five: self-belief

THE JEWS WHO left Egypt with Moshe Rabbeinu had already seen a great deal. They had witnessed how ten incredible plagues systematically destroyed the mightiest and most arrogant nation on the face of the earth at that time. They had watched the Red Sea split for them, and then drown the pursuing Egyptian army. They ate bread from Heaven while a miraculous well accompanied them everywhere to take care of all their water needs.

But the peak of all experiences was actually hearing God speak and give Torah at Mt. Sinai. This is incomprehensible to us, and it is an example of how much God cared for the Jewish people and how great a miracle He was prepared to perform for them. You would think that if any people should have perfect faith and trust in God, it would have been that generation of Jews.

Yet it says about them:

> Because you did not believe in God and did not trust in His salvation. (Tehillim 78:22)

> Nevertheless, they sinned further and had no faith in His wonders. (Tehillim 78:32).

They did not believe in God after all He had done for them? They did not have faith in His wonders after all they had seen? How is that even possible? The Leshem explains:

> However, this was not due to an evil heart, God forbid, but because they did not find themselves worthy of this...Therefore, instead, they constantly complained, "Why did you bring us up from Egypt?" since they saw that they could not maintain the proper faith in God because of the yetzer hara that kept overcoming them and renewing itself each day. (Drushei Olam HaTohu, Chelek 2, Drush 5, Anaf 4, Siman 3)

In other words, the Jewish people who left Egypt with Moshe Rabbeinu DEFINITELY did believe in God. Furthermore, they most CERTAINLY did not question God's ability to do ANYTHING He wanted for them. The only thing they questioned was their own worthiness to receive such Divine Providence, and in doubting themselves they doubted God.

This is a HUGE point. It's a huge point because bitachon and emunah—trust and faith in God—is a HUGE point. It's everything, because it is the true measure of any relationship, but especially of the relationship between a person and God. That is because we're only as close to another person as we feel we can trust him or her.

If we doubt the existence of God, or question the extent to which He gets involved in our life, we will naturally be weak in our trust in God. But the generation of the desert didn't have these doubts. Rather they were weak in bitachon and emunah because they didn't believe in themselves. Was that a soul thing, or a function of the klipos?

We've already said that the soul can do no wrong, even for the "right" reasons. In the previous chapter we identified the soul as "Ish Emes," the "Person of Truth." Ya'akov Avinu exemplified this trait because he lived his life as a soul, after "defeating" his klipah. This earned him the name

"Yisroel." "Ya'akov" was the twin of "Eisav," but "Yisroel" is in a spiritual league of its own.

If so, then self-doubt is not soul-doubt, but a doubt that originates from, and is perpetuated by, a person's klipah. It uses the concept of humility AGAINST the person, as it likes to do. If the klipah doesn't get a person to fall through sin, then it will try to do it through "mitzvah" instead.

This is called the "frum[1] yetzer hara." A mitzvah performed inappropriately is a sin. Eat well, but not on a fast day. Give tzedakah, but not to an evil cause. Learn Torah, but not to the point that it interferes with other mitzvos. Be humble, but not the point that it interferes with your service of God.

That was the source of Shaul HaMelech's downfall. One of the reasons he was chosen as the first king of the Jewish people was because of his humility. But his humility was also the cause of his loss of the kingship:

> Shmuel said, "Even if you are small in your own eyes, are you not the head of the tribes of Israel?" (I Shmuel 15:17)

A soul, by definition, is humble. It is pure

---

[1] A yiddish word that means "religious."

truth, a spark of Divine Light. It can't be anything else. But as we learn from Moshe Rabbeinu, called by God Himself "the humblest man on the earth,"[2] there are times when it is "truthful" to be passive, and there are times when truth demands that a person be aggressive.

Being humble is about doing what is truthful, for the most part at ANY cost.[3] It is about being more devoted to the bigger picture than the smaller one. Sometimes that may mean looking out for yourself first. Other times it means putting personal needs second, or third, whatever the moment requires according to the direction of Torah.

Humility can never interfere with another mitzvah. If it does, it is the klipah distorting it to intimidate us from doing what God wants us to do, which is what it did to the Jews in the desert. What difference does perceived unworthiness make if God tells us to do something? Part of the celebration of any redemption is how it happened in spite of our lack of worth.

Besides, who really knows who is worthy and who is not? Just as we cannot judge other people

---

[2] Bamidbar 12:7-8.

[3] Sometimes a "cost" can require an adjustment in action because of the ULTIMATE truth, as when God changed Sarah's words to protect Avraham (Bereishis 18:13).

because we are unaware of their past and their challenges, likewise we have a difficult time judging ourselves properly as well. Instead, we're just supposed to figure out what we CAN do to meet a challenge, and leave the rest of the details up to God.

In any given situation you could really just ask yourself, "What would a soul say in a situation like this?" Or "What would the klipah say at such a moment?" You could even use this idea to make a card game for children. "You want to speak loshon hara about your friend, and you feel you have good reason to. What would your soul say? What would the klipah say?" This could be a multiple choice game, and it would be VERY instructive.

Consider losing your temper, for example. Sometimes it is OBVIOUSLY wrong, but often it seems justified at the time. Later, after the situation has passed and the temper has cooled, feelings of regret may follow in the wake. It's as if a little voice emerges WAY too late, saying, "You didn't have to get so angry about that!"

Guilt-ridden, the klipah may argue back and say, "Yes, I did," but usually in a much lamer voice. Certainly as time goes on, the voice of reason gets stronger until, after a while, you can't even remember why it was such a big deal at the time.

If only we could freeze-frame each moment

as the crisis unfolds. The only thing that would have to keep working in real time would be our brain. Then we could study the situation in detail and have enough time to be calm enough to ask, "What is my soul saying at this moment, and what is the klipah yelling back?"

The soul also demands "justice, truth, and liberty for all," but in the ULTIMATE sense. It knows that what seems like justice, truth, or liberty on the surface can be just the opposite once all the facts are in. Hence, the rabbis have advised us to be deliberate in judgment.[4]

The klipos don't really care about justice, truth, and liberty for anyone else but themselves. That being the case, how true can their definitions of any of these words actually be? In any event, that will not stop them from arguing that they really are interested only in the real thing.

Unfortunately, we cannot freeze the moments. They come and go quite quickly, and many catch us by surprise. They happen, we react, and we only get to think about them after the fact—sometimes after irreparable damage has occurred.

There are two possible solutions. The first is to take the advice of the rabbis and learn how not

------

[4] Pirkei Avos 1:1.

to respond immediately to a crisis. We're not talking about taking time to apply first aid to a person in need. We're talking about taking time to better evaluate a situation and custom design our response so that it is appropriate and productive.

The second solution is preparation. A fundamental of Torah living is that everything requires preparation, Shabbos being the prime example.[5] When NASA sent men into space, they prepared for various scenarios that might occur, so that they would know what to do to avoid disaster.

The same thing is true with S.W.A.T. teams, and Navy Seals. Not panicking at a moment's notice can mean the difference between a successful mission and one that fails miserably. If trained in advance, the brain can remain calm, and allow a person to keep in step with the overall reality, not just the initially perceived one.

Believe it or not, this is really what Purim comes to remind us each year, as the following parable portrays:

> Once there were two yeshivah boys who grew up together in the early 1800s. They played together, learned together, and did just

---

5 Avodah Zarah 3a.

about everything they could together. However, many years later when it was time to marry, their fathers arranged shidduchim to women who lived on opposite sides of Europe. Since travel at that time was slow and expensive, and mail delivery was unreliable, it did not take long for the newly married men to forget about each other. Years passed, and one day they both had occasion to travel. As Divine Providence would have it, each man passed through the Vienna train station on his way home at the same time, although headed in opposite directions. As they made their way to their respective trains in Vienna, they "happened" to pass each other on the platform. At first they didn't recognize each other: over the years black, scraggly beards had given way to full, gray beards. They were mature leaders now, and each looked the part. But as they nonchalantly passed each other, each froze in his tracks. Instinctively, they slowly turned until they faced each other.

"Dovid, is that you?" Moshe asked incredulously.

"Moshe, can that be you? Dovid asked, choking up.

Suddenly, in the middle of a crowded Vienna train station, the two men dropped their valises and embraced each other. Remaining in their embrace as they walked, as if letting go would mean instant separation for another 25 years, they made their way to a bench.

"Moshe!" Dovid exclaimed. "I've heard so much about you. I've heard you've made a real name for yourself in learning. How's your wife and how is your family? What are you up to these days?"

"And you!" Moshe interrupted. "I hear that you are a Rosh Yeshivah now. I always knew you'd be one someday."

Then, all of a sudden, a train whistle blew, the first warning that it was time to board their respective trains. Dovid and Moshe looked at each other, and asked,

"Which way are you going?"

"West! And you?"

"East!"

"No, it can't be! How can 25 years of separation can come down to a few minutes of reunion?" Moshe asked tearfully.

"Wait!" said Dovid, smiling. "I have an idea. I have wine in my bag and two glasses. Why don't you take a glass of wine and bring it to the conductor of your train? I'll do the same with mine. We'll get them drunk and then no one will go anywhere for at least an hour. Then we can catch up on everything that has happened since we last left the shtetl!"[6]

This story was told in response to the question, "Why drink on Purim?" It was meant as an analogy, the two men representing the souls of two people, and the conductors of the trains representing their bodies. Giving wine to their respective "conductors" is like giving wine to our bodies on Purim, to "neutralize" them enough so that souls, on Purim, can have a chance to relate to one another as souls.

That's how we first come into the world, as souls "stuck in bodies," you know, as "souls having a physical experience." We were pure and we were connected to the world as souls, and to other souls as well.

Then we grew up. A body is needy. It loves to experience the pleasures of the world, which are so visible and so available. Bodily functions we never asked for kicked in, and the next thing we knew, we were being forced to service the demands of the body.

With age came increased responsibility and

---

[6] This was told to me in the name of Rabbi Yitzchak Hutner, zt"l.

opportunity, and lots of worries as well. It was if layer upon layer were being piled on top of the soul until its voice became so muffled that it was easy to forget it was in there in the first place. At that point we learned to relate to ourselves as physical beings, and to others the same way. The "conductor" was clearly in control.

We can't get drunk everyday, and it's even questionable about how drunk one should get on Purim.[7] It's not about LOSING da'as,[8] but rather about GAINING it. The wine is just meant to be a means to remind us that our "conductors" CAN be neutralized, so that we can go through life more as souls, as our TRUE selves.

How? That needs a chapter of its own.

---

[7] Yesod v'Shoresh HaAvodah, Purim.
[8] Usually "da'as" is translated as "knowledge," but in this case, it is more like consciousness and spiritual awareness.

TO BETTER UNDERSTAND the soul, it is important to know what it is. What is its essence? Yes, it is Divine Light, but what does that mean?

On the first day of Creation, God made light. It is clear, however, that THIS light was not physical like that of a sun or a light bulb. The sun was not put in place until the fourth day of Creation, and light bulbs were not invented for another 5,000-plus years.

Not only that, but the Talmud says that with this light, Adam HaRishon was able to see from ONE END of the world to the OTHER END.[1] The

---

[1] Chagigah 12a.

light we're used to might enable us to see a distance of a few miles, but we can't even see around a corner.

Furthermore, the Talmud says that this original light didn't last past the first day of Creation. God hid it almost as fast as He created it, because He "saw" how evil people in the future would abuse it.[2] The light WE use has been accessible to "good" and "bad" alike from the very beginning.

Where do you HIDE such a light (appropriately called the "Ohr HaGanuz," or "the Hidden Light")? Even sunlight is hard to hide, and usually requires a person to hide from it. How does a light hide from man?

The starting point is in knowing that "reality" is multi-layered. There is the PHYSICAL REALITY with which we interact daily, and higher levels of consciousness in which we believe but cannot see. If we interact with them, we can't SEE how. A person can pray to change a situation, but how can he know if it was HIS prayer that actually changed it? However, just because we can't SEE the invisible layers of reality in action does not mean that we do not KNOW what they are or how they work.

By now most people are familiar with the

---

[2] Rashi, Bereishis 1:4.

universe. They know it exists, that they are an infinitesimally small part of it, and that it is MASSIVE beyond comprehension, 93 billion light-years wide[3] to be more precise. That's BIG, and yet it is a pinhead in size in comparison to the NON-observable universe, of which most believing people know only in the most general terms.

The universe WE know is at the "bottom" of all "worlds," in a spiritual dimension called "Asiyah." This name comes from the Hebrew word that means "to do," or "to make," because it is the world in which man does and makes things. It is the world of human action, and it is the most PHYSICAL level of reality created.

The next level up from Asiyah is called "Yetzirah," which means "formation." It is a stage of creating during which things are "formed" from pre-existing "materials," similar to a table of wood that a carpenter makes from a pre-existing tree, or a vase that a potter makes with clay from the ground. It is the "creation" of SOMETHING FROM SOMETHING.

Yetzirah, Kabbalah explains, is the basis of our 6,000 years of history. History may seem random, but the potential of every moment and every thing was "rooted" in the level of Yetzirah

---

[3] This refers to the observable universe.

LONG before they themselves came into existence.[4]

"Beriyah" is the world above Yetzirah. Yetzirah is "formation," but Beriyah is "creation," which is SOMETHING FROM NOTHING, otherwise known as "ex nihilo."

Long ago scientists questioned whether or not the universe had a beginning. They did not know how the universe originated or even IF it originated, so they just assumed it didn't. Then, in 1925, the astronomer Edwin Hubble proved that the universe is expanding, which meant it must have had a beginning. Scientists decided to call that beginning the "Big Bang."[5]

The only question is what created the Big Bang. It could not have been SOMETHING, because then you'd have to figure out what created the original something that gave rise to the Big

---

[4] The 6,000 years are the sum of the spans of six sefiros: Chesed, Gevurah, Tifferes, Netzach, Hod, and Yesod. The sefiros are spiritual entities through which Divine Light flows to make and maintain Creation as per the will of God (Drushei Olam HaTohu, Chelek 2, Drush 4, Anaf 18, Siman 6).

[5] The Big Bang is a scientific theory about how the universe started, and then made the stars and galaxies we see today. The universe began as a very hot, small, dense super-force (the mix of the four fundamental forces), with no stars, atoms, form, or structure (called a "singularity"). Wikipedia

Bang. But what else is there besides something?

Nothing.

NOTHING?

Yes. Scientists concluded that nothing created the universe! And the last time we checked, they were still trying to figure out what "nothing" actually is, and how it can create ANYTHING, let alone an entire universe.

Torah doesn't have this problem. It agrees that everything came from "nothing," but it already knows what the "nothing" is. Creation ex nihilo does not reveal it, but Creation being "Yaish m'Ayin," the Hebrew of "something from nothing," does.

The first thing to recall is that God is not only infinite, but He is infinitely SPIRITUAL. Man is also spiritual, and angels even more so. But no created entity will EVER come even remotely close to God's level of transcendence. Relatively speaking, compared to everything created, God is SO spiritual that it seems as if He does not exist. Hence He is also called "Ayin," which means "nothing."[6]

So when the Torah talks about Creation being "m'Ayin," it means from a COMPLETELY spiritual realm. That is the level of Atzilus, the second highest dimension, and the first to be COMPLETELY

---

[6] Drushei Olam HaTohu, Chelek 2, Drush 5, Anaf 4, Siman 3.

spiritual and godly. It emanates light down to create and maintain the physical world, but the light itself is completely spiritual.

As spiritual and as godly as Atzilus is, it is still not the highest level of existence. There is one level higher, and even though it is discussed in Kabbalah, we know very little about it. Whatever is known is from reverse-engineering Atzilus, similar to understanding a father through his son.

Called "Adam Kadmon," literally "Ancient

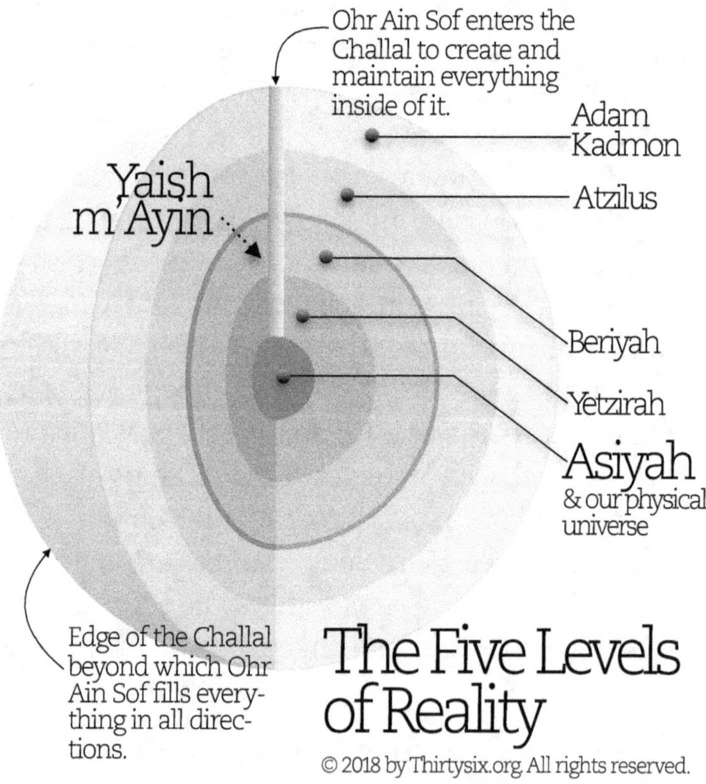

The Five Levels of Reality

Man," it was the first creation, long before any physical man was created. Adam Kadmon is SO spiritual and sublime that human minds cannot comprehend it, and it is also called "Ayin."

Beyond Adam Kadmon is "Ohr Ain Sof," the "Light without End." This is the light that created everything, and still does. It surrounds the "challal"[7] within which all five dimensions exist, and continues out in EVERY direction, INFINITELY.

It is this "chain of command" that made Creation possible, and which maintains existence. It is the system that God created to filter His light and implement His will from moment to moment for all of history.

But how does one access these higher levels of reality? Why is it even necessary? Because of a direct correlation between the five levels of reality and our five levels of soul. Although we have

Five Levels of Reality	Five Levels of Soul
Adam Kadmon	Yechidah
Atzilus	Chayah
Beriyah	Neshamah
Yetzirah	Ruach
Asiyah	Nefesh

---

[7] "Hollow," the Kabbalistic name for the "space" within the Ohr Ain Sof Creation exists.

only ONE soul, it has FIVE parts, and they correspond to the five levels of reality.[8] When people ascend to higher levels of consciousness, they also go "deeper" into their soul.

It is, of course, not as simple as it sounds. Generally, those who pursue spiritual growth and a greater understanding of Torah will "naturally" ascend through the levels of soul. Kabbalah, however, addresses the issue in a more specific manner,[9] which allows them to more precisely pursue their goal of finding their soul-self.

Having outlined this, it is possible to answer where the original light of Creation, the Ohr Ha-Ganuz, was hidden. It wasn't so much HIDDEN as it was WITHDRAWN, back up to its source within the system, on a level within Adam Kadmon. It is "hidden" inasmuch as we have no means to access it at this stage of history.[10] But if we could access it, we would be able to know our soul on the most profound levels.

Maybe we still can. The Torah says:

God saw that the light was good, and God

---

[8] See my book "Reincarnation Again."
[9] Sha'ar HaGilgulim, Introduction 18.
[10] Drushei Olam HaTohu, Drush Aitz HaDa'as; Hakdamos u'Sha'arim, Sha'ar 6, Ch. 10-11.

separated between the light and the darkness. (Bereishis 1:4)

He saw that the wicked were unworthy of using it, and therefore set it apart for the righteous in the Future Time. (Rashi)

He made a separation in the illumination of the light, that it should not flow or give off light except for the righteous, whose actions DRAW IT DOWN and make it shine. However, the actions of the evil BLOCK it, leaving them in darkness. This itself was the hiding of the light. (Sefer HaKlallim, Klal 18, Anaf 8, Os 4)

One advantage of spiritual realities is that they can be both close and far away at the same time. Overlapping one another, they are close to one another. Closed off from the spiritually unworthy, they might as well be billions of light years away from each other. Becoming spiritually worthy enables people to gain access to incredible worlds and self-knowledge without having to physically go anywhere at all.[11]

Now we come to the main point. True, a righteous life leads to more reward in the World-

---

[11] See Tosfos, Chagigah 14b: Four who entered Pardes.

to-Come. True, a righteous life greatly enhances the spiritual quality of a person's time in this world. But the most "selfish" reason for a life of Torah is greater SOUL-knowledge, and there is absolutely NOTHING more fulfilling than THIS.

WTC DOES NOT stand for "World Trade Center," at least not in this context. It stands for "World-to-Come," otherwise known as "Olam HaBa" in Hebrew. And although it may seem overly mystical and a long way off, it has light to shed on the story of the soul, and vice-versa.

The Talmud makes a fascinating statement:

Yud-Heh…refers to the two worlds which The Holy One, Blessed is He, created, one with the letter Heh and the other with the letter Yud. (Menachos 29b)

Kabbalah explains how God used the Aleph-

Bais to make Creation. Although the letters of other languages are mostly just conventions created to facilitate language, the Aleph-Bais has the deepest of secrets encoded into its letters.

For example, the first letter, Aleph, is comprised of two Yuds joined by a Vav. The numerical value of a Yud is 10, so two Yuds have a value of 20. The numerical value of the letter Vav is six, giving 26 as the total of the three parts of the Aleph. This is also the gematria of God's four-letter name, the "Shem Hovayah," and the  Aleph, whose value is one, alludes to God, Who is One.

Thus, although it may be difficult to conceive of making ANY kind of world from just a single letter, Kabbalah details exactly how it happened. That's not the Talmud's question though. It asks this instead:

> I do not know whether the future world was created with the Yud and this world with the Heh, or this world with the Yud and the future world with the Heh. (Menachos 29b)

Torah tradition speaks about two worlds, the

physical, temporal one in which we live, and which will last 6,000 years, and a future one that is completely spiritual and will last forever. The first is called "Olam HaZeh," or "This World," and the future eternal one is called "Olam HaBa," or "The World-to-Come."

Regarding these two worlds it says:

> This world is like a corridor before the World-to-Come. Rectify yourself in the corridor in order to be able to enter the banquet hall. (Pirkei Avos 4:16)

The question is which letter God used to create which world. The answer is known from Kabbalah, but the Talmud found a verse from the Torah's account of Creation that alludes to it as well:

> It is written, "These are the generations of the heaven and of the earth when they were created—b'hibaram" (Bereishis 2:4). Don't read it as "b'hibaram—when they were created," but as "b'Heh bera'am—He created them with a Heh... (Menachos 29b)

The letters of "b'hibaram" are Bais-HEH-Bais-Raish-Mem. But if the word is divided into two parts, which is legal for drush purposes, especially if there is a tradition to support the idea, the word can be read "b'HEH—with a Heh"..."baram—He created them," referring to all the components of Creation. Thus the Talmud concludes, God used the letter Heh to make this world and, therefore, the letter Yud to make Olam HaBa.

The Talmud also explains why the letter Heh was the right letter for this world, which has something to do with making teshuvah[1] possible. It is the Maharal who explains why the letter Yud was most appropriate as the basis of the World-to-Come, and it has everything to do with a discussion about the soul.[2]

Every letter save one in the Aleph-Bais is actually a composite of other letters, as seen above with the Aleph. The only letter for which this is not the case is the Yud, which is comprised of a Yud and nothing more.

This is highly significant, the Maharal explains. It represents what he calls "pashtus," which means "simplicity." But not just any pashtus, but rather the pashtus of Olam HaBa, the kind that is associated with God Himself. Olam HaZeh is a composite of MANY things, and life is quite com-

---

[1] Repentance.
[2] Haggadah Shel Pesach; Ner Mitzvah.

plex. Olam HaBa is not complex at all, existing on a level of sublime unity known only on the level of the soul.

This difference creates tension in life. Our body likes the complexity of life, as is evident from all the gadgets we create and purchase. But the soul loves pashtus, as is evident from how peaceful we are when we find it, perhaps from watching a sun set, or waves going back and forth, or being cut off from society on a camping trip in the woods.

But there is a much higher level of pashtus. Obviously the more an activity resembles the world of the Yud, the world of Olam HaBa, the more pashut the pashtus will be. And, there is nothing more like this than the four levels of Torah.

The kabbalistic name for the four levels of Torah is "Pardes." The word itself means "orchard," but the Hebrew spelling—Peh-Raish-Dalet-Samech—refers to an "orchard" of a different nature. It is an acronym for the four levels of Torah, from the most obvious to the most sublime: Pshat, Remez, Drush, and Sod.[3]

---

[3] Sha'ar HaGilgulim, Introduction 11. Translated, the levels are Simple, Hint, Exegetical, and Secret. Examples of each category of a Torah verse, Mishnah, Talmud, and Kabbalah.

As one delves deeper into Torah, he ascends levels of consciousness. Just as the five worlds correspond to the five levels of soul, the first four levels of Torah learning correspond to the four lower levels of reality and soul:

	Adam Kadmon	Yechidah
Sod	Atzilus	Chayah
Drush	Beriyah	Neshamah
Remez	Yetzirah	Ruach
Pshat	Asiyah	Nefesh
Four Levels of Torah	Five Levels of Reality	Five Levels of Soul

All three areas are interconnected, and whatever happens in one realm impacts the other two. Therefore, as people deepen their knowledge of Torah, going from Pshat to Remez to Drush, and finally to Sod, they ascend from Asiyah to Yetzirah to Beriyah, and finally to Atzilus.

As people advance from Pshat to Remez, they go from a less spiritual realm to a more spiritual one. The difference will be noticeable, but not as much as when they go from Remez to Drush, from Mishnah to Talmud.

As the Leshem[4] explains, entering the realm of pure Kabbalah is the greatest leap of all, "m'yaish l'Ayin":

> The rest of the areas of Torah learning are clothed in matters of this world, which is not the case with Kabbalah, particularly the words of the Arizal, who built upon the Ideres and Sifra d'Tzniusa,[5] and the other secret sections of the holy Zohar. All of its matters deal only on the level of Atzilus and the worlds of the light of Ain Sof.[6] That is why the wisdom of Kabbalah is called "Nistar—Hidden…" (Drushei Olam HaTohu, Chelek 1, Drush 5, Siman 7, Os 8)

In other words, as people deepen their knowledge of Torah, they remove layers of "clothing" from the "soul" of Torah. The light of Torah becomes less filtered, more like Olam HaBa, as people learn Kabbalah properly, according to tradition, with the proper background and above all, with the proper level of purity and emunah.

---

[4] The great kabbalist Rabbi Shlomo Elyashiv (1841-1926).

[5] Two very kabbalistic and technical parts of the Zohar dealing with the process of Creation.

[6] God's infinite light.

After all, if Kabbalah is the level of Atzilus, and Atzilus is a level of Olam HaBa, then truly entering Sod is like entering Olam HaBa. Unlike the lower levels of Torah, learning Kabbalah is about a lot more than just reading the words and understanding the ideas. You CERTAINLY can't get into Olam HaBa without first fulfilling the proper spiritual criteria, as is the case with Kabbalah, as mentioned previously:

> He made a separation in the illumination of the light, that it should not flow or give off light except for the righteous, whose actions DRAW IT DOWN and make it shine. However, the actions of the evil BLOCK it, leaving them in darkness. This itself was the hiding of the light. (Sefer HaKlallim, Klal 18, Anaf 8, Os 4)

Even on lesser levels of knowledge, ideas have to "click." Many times we can read something and even explain the words, but the ideas do not resonate with us until after we have thought about them for a while. It might be a simple matter of asking a few questions and getting answers, or of having an experience that sheds light on the new ideas.

Kabbalah is unlike any other knowledge available to man. It requires more than just brains to fathom. It also requires a certain spiritual intuition that does not come naturally, but rather with a very specific spiritual development. Without it, the wisest geniuses can learn Kabbalah as intently as possible, and still not be able to "unify" with the knowledge, which is essential for understanding it as it is meant to be understood.

This spiritual sensitivity is what the Maharal calls "pashtus," and he explains that it is what matzah alludes to. Made only of flour and water, the minimal number of components to make an edible dish, it is "pashut" compared to all other foods, which are far more complex. And THIS, the Maharal explains, is the basis of human freedom. It is when people get absorbed in the material complexities of life that they become enslaved by them.

This enslavement was Mitzrayim, both then and in every generation since. This word was translated as "Egypt" and still is, because it was the FIRST Mitzrayim. Egypt is the Torah's name for the nation that once lived on the land which is now called Egypt.

However, the word "Egypt" is actually a composite of two Hebrew words: "meitzer," which means "boundary," and "yum,"[7] which is spelled

---

[7] Drushei Olam HaTohu, Chelek 2, Drush 5, Anaf 4, Siman 3.

Yud-Mem and has the gematria of 50—an allusion to the "Nun Sha'arei Binah," the "Fifty Gates of Understanding." Technically speaking, any society that "constricts" the Nun Sha'arei Binah has the spiritual status of "Mitzrayim," ANYWHERE in the world, at ANY TIME in history.

It is obvious that the "understanding" part is talking about knowledge. But what are the "fifty gates," and where exactly are they?

The truth is that although the Talmud refers to them,[8] it doesn't explain what they are. Kabbalah discusses them in many places and in explicit detail, but it requires background to understand what it says.

On a simple level, the Fifty Gates of Understanding are the basis of all Torah knowledge. It is Divine Light from the level of Binah, which is the level of Beriyah. This means that it is less "filtered" compared to "secular" knowledge, which is why it promotes a relationship with God as opposed to distracting from it.

As the Midrash teaches, Torah was the blueprint for Creation.[9] Thus ALL knowledge has to exist within it, and it does.[10] It's just that Torah

---

8 Rosh Hashanah 21b.

9 Bereishis Rabbah 2:4.

10 Pirkei Avos 5:26.

knowledge provides access to the SOURCE of the knowledge higher up in the system, and "secular" knowledge is what it looks like after the light has been filtered level after level on its way down to the World of Asiyah.

Another way of looking at this is vis-à-vis the Tree of Life and the Tree of Knowledge of Good and Evil. On the surface of it, they are two entirely different trees. But, as Kabbalah explains, both trees originated from the same source, and eventually the Tree of Knowledge of Good and Evil will be transformed into the Tree of Life.

In the meantime, however, the knowledge of the Tree of Knowledge of Good and Evil has "watered down" Torah so much that it is possible to learn it and still not feel connected to God. The knowledge of the Tree of Life is a revelation of Divine Light on a much higher level, making it a direct link to God Himself.

A materialistic society such as Egypt was only interested in knowledge that furthered the cause of materialism. Therefore, while the people pursued the knowledge of the Tree of Knowledge of Good and Evil, they rejected the knowledge of the Tree of Life, and did everything they could to make the Jews do the same thing.

THAT is how a nation at any point in history becomes a "meitzer-yum," a Mitzrayim, a constrictor of the Fifty Gates of Understanding. "All" it has to do is become overly materialistic, especially at the cost of spirituality. In today's very complex and materialistic world, Mitzrayim basically spans many borders, having become an international community.

Righteous people live the opposite kind of life. They have minimal physical possessions, which for non-righteous people would be considered poverty. However, given that their communities would gladly support most of them, it is clear that righteous people CHOOSE their minimalist existence because of its pashtus.

To "outsiders," meaning those who have not reached such a high level of spiritual greatness—even if they are religious—such a life of abstinence looks like, well, just a life of abstinence. These outsiders can't "see" how such a life can bring more pleasure than what can be enjoyed from a physically more complex and material existence.

The principle is that the more people are able to derive SPIRITUAL pleasure from life, the less they feel a need for PHYSICAL pleasures. It's hard to believe this when spiritual pleasures are seemingly not readily available, whereas material pleasures are apparently in abundance. But it certainly becomes a lot clearer after having experienced spiritual pleasure.

In a metaphoric AND literal sense, physical pleasures are only skin deep. Spiritual pleasures, on the other hand, are SOUL deep, because they are intellectually and emotionally meaningful. They are a function of some higher value in life, such as doing good for others, or even just enjoying a family relationship, and these pleasures "nourish" our soul.

The amazing thing is how both can occur simultaneously—the spiritual pleasure and the physical one—and enhance each other. This is the lesson of Shabbos, that commands us to physically enjoy ourselves—not for self-gratification but in honor of Shabbos. It just makes life "taste" better.

This is the deeper meaning of the following story:

> The emperor asked Rebi Yehoshua ben Chanania, "Why does Shabbos food have such a fragrant smell?"
>
> "We have a certain seasoning called 'Shabbos' that we put into it," he told him, "and that gives it a fragrant smell."
>
> "Give us some of it," he said.
>
> "It only works for a person who observes Shabbos," he explained. "It does not work for a person who does not observe Shabbos."

(Shabbos 119a)

It wasn't a physical spice that Rebi Yehoshua was talking about. If it were, the emperor could have forced him to reveal what it was. Rebi Yehoshua was talking about a mentality, a SHABBOS mentality, and that has to be built by the person himself through the proper ideas and activities in life.

It is not for no reason that Shabbos is called "one-sixtieth of the World-to-Come."[11] After six days of complexity, it is a day of pashtus. After a week of material pursuit, Shabbos is a day of material retreat. Clearly this does not mean abstention from material pleasures, evident from the halachos themselves. It means material pleasures for the sake of spiritual growth.

In fact, reward in the World-to-Come is not simply recompense for a life of self-sacrifice solely for the sake of self-sacrifice in this world. It is the automatic result of having pursued the pashtus of Olam HaBa in Olam HaZeh. To BE a "Ben Olam HaBa," someone worthy of going to the World-to-Come, you have to BECOME one NOW, by being someone for whom pashtus is more liberating and enjoyable than material gain.

---

[11] Brochos 57b.

The good news is that this is who we REALLY are, in essence. It is the way we were made. And it is what the Torah brings out in us, or more accurately, OUT of us. The rest of life, after accepting this idea, is for living with its reality.

DO YOU BELIEVE in the World-to-Come? I mean, REALLY believe, with ALL your heart? Before you answer that question, please keep reading.

When the Talmud[1] speaks about the World-to-Come, henceforth "WTC," it refers to the place that "no eye has even seen except for God's."[2] The Maharal[3] says that this is the reason such a central concept as the WTC is not mentioned in the Torah. The Torah is prophecy—what Moshe

---

[1] Brochos 34b.

[2] Yeshayahu 64:4.

[3] Rabbi Yehudah Loew ben Betzalel (1520–1609).

Rabbeinu was able to envision—and that did not include Olam HaBa.[4]

The Leshem discusses the various stages of the WTC, but mostly in terms of the shifting positions of the sefiros as Creation reverses itself. History has moved away from God, which is why people can deny His existence. Once Moshiach comes, Creation will start moving back in the direction of its Source, becoming increasingly more spiritual as it does. But what does that mean for us?

The Zohar is more explicit about what it is going to look like in the WTC, and what will happen once we get there. The work "Yesod v'Shoresh HaAvodah" relies on these sources to encourage people to work hard in life to earn a place there. But it is not clear whether or not the Zohar is to be taken literally, or if it is just speaking about the unknown in familiar terms.

The truth is that we have no idea what to expect after 6000, and it is VERY hard to relate to something you know nothing about. We're the proof of that. People push themselves to the point of exhaustion to get a degree that they hope will earn them a good living, or to excel at an activity in the hope of receiving great reward for their

---

[4] Gevuros Hashem.

success. But when it comes to earning reward in the WTC, we'd rather take it easy and save our strength for things we can relate to.

Imagine an elderly woman asking you for a simple favor, like helping her load the car with some groceries. Then, after you help, she gives you a check for $5 million. Wouldn't you think that the check is a joke and the woman is crazy?

"No, it's real," she tells you, noticing your astonishment. "Take it to the bank and cash it. You'll see."

Stunned, you ask, barely getting the words out of your mouth, "But what's it for?"

"For helping me get my groceries to my car, obviously."

Unsure of whether or not you are dreaming, you further ask, "But how is that worth SO much money to you?" wondering if your benefactor has lost her marbles.

"It just is," she answers, getting in her car. "Thanks again," she says as she drives off, leaving you with your mouth wide open and your brain short-circuiting."

What's the analogy? Let's go a little further.

Years back I wondered why Bill Gates was able to earn so much money. "Why do you ask?" people replied. "He developed a product everyone wanted, and made a killing from it. Steve Jobs too, and all the other incredibly rich people in the world. That's the beauty of capitalism," they told me.

"Of course," I said. "On a simplistic level, that is 100 percent true. But," I explained, "lots of people develop great ideas and work really hard to turn them into money-making successes, but fail. Often the person with the idea does not succeed, and the second one to develop it does. Why? Obviously mazal[5] plays a role, and something else as well…"

Then one day, around the time that all kinds of Torah institutions began taking advantage of the internet to further the cause of Torah, it occurred to me. I suddenly realized how much computers developed by Apple and programs developed by Microsoft have helped many of us to develop Torah ideas and share them with others.

The computer age, for many reasons now, has greatly helped the spreading of Torah. Thanks to Amazon, I can publish books at a rate I never could before. Thanks to their data base, I have a far larger market than I could ever have had on my own. And thanks to the great penchant for improvement, they provide me and many other

____

[5] Personal destiny as "encoded" in the constellations (Shabbos 156a).

teachers of Torah with excellent marketing reports and insights, basically for free.

Now, I know what you're probably thinking. You're probably thinking that I am being awfully presumptuous to think that THEIR wealth is because of ME. And it WOULD be presumptuous, but that's not what I am saying. I am saying that this is the case because of TORAH, and if THAT sounds presumptuous, then you should read even further.

First of all, one of the first things Rashi says at the beginning of his Torah commentary is that the whole WORLD was made for Torah. He bases himself upon the verse itself and the Midrash. This means that whatever happens in history, every last detail of it and no matter how distant it seems from ANY Torah purpose, is for the sake of Torah.

How far does this idea go? The Talmud discusses this as well. It portrays how, on the final day of judgment, God will judge ALL the nations. Rome, being the mightiest (at least at the time of the Talmud), will go first.

When God will ask the Romans, "Nu, how did you justify YOUR existence?" they will claim that everything they built was just to allow the Jewish people to learn Torah. God will snap back at them and say, "World-class fools! Everything you built was for your own benefit!" and off they will go, head hanging down,[6] as will all the other nations that try to pull the same shtik.

It is the Brisker Rav who pointed out something very telling. He asked why God only called them fools, and not liars. The reason, he answers, is because they really weren't liars. Everything they did ended up being for the sake of the Jewish people and Torah, as Rashi explains in Chumash. But they were FOOLS for thinking that they could convince God that this had been their intention all along.

However, as the Talmud points out, God does not let any kindness go unrewarded, even if it wasn't intended to be a kindness. If it did good anyhow, the person or nation that did it has to be rewarded in some way,[7] so that God will "owe" them nothing when history comes to an end. If they're not going to the World-to-Come, then they have to be paid off in this world.[8]

Even if they ARE going to go to the WTC, they can still get rewarded here. Only the Jewish people have to wait until the WTC to receive their reward for mitzvos,[9] making what they receive in this

---

[6] Avodah Zarah 2b.
[7] Bava Kamma 38b; Rashi, Pesachim 22a.
[8] Kiddushin 40b; Avodah Zarah 10b.
[9] Kiddushin 39b; Avodah Zarah.

world "tzedakah."[10] Non-Jews can receive reward in this world as well, but since they are not commanded in mitzvos, they don't receive as much reward for them as one who IS commanded.[11]

Which brings us back to people like Bill Gates and those like him. Of course they would find this silly, ridiculous, perhaps even offensive. THEIR success was for the sake of TORAH? What about their genius...self-sacrifice...their...their...

Go ahead. Make a list. But for every reason you come up with to explain why THEY have been so successful, there are millions of others who have done the exact same thing, but have not even come close financially to people like Bill Gates, Steve Jobs, Jeff Bizos, etc. This is God's doing, and as the Torah and Talmud state, it is for the sake of Torah.

But we just said that a person who is commanded to do a mitzvah and does it is rewarded more than one who does a mitzvah he has no obligation to do! Then why are these unwitting supporters of Torah so abundantly rewarded?

Therein lies the crux of the matter. The only reason why we can even ASK this question is because of how LITTLE we know about the WORTH

---

[10] Brochos 17a.
[11] Kiddushin 30a.

of a mitzvah. If we knew better, we'd be asking instead, "WHAT? HE ONLY RECEIVED 137 BILLION DOLLARS FOR INCIDENTALLY SUPPORTING TORAH?"

This is probably WHY God is giving people who support Torah so much money. We're so in the dark about Olam HaBa that we treat mitzvos EXTREMELY casually. We know that Olam HaBa is coming, but we have nothing in human experience with which to compare it, so we don't know that we're going to get something like that, and even more.

When we get up in the morning and wash "Neggel Vasser,"[12] how much reward do we get? What about when we wash our hands before eating bread? How about for praying, or any of the other mitzvos we might do throughout the course of a day, week, or life? And what about special mitzvos like Shabbos? What's the reward for them?

Who knows? One thing, however, is for certain. Whatever the reward is, it is SO great that there is no way to really receive it in this world. We're not even equipped to enjoy THAT much

---

[12] "Night Water." This is the special washing of the hands from a cup upon waking up in the morning, at least three times alternately on each hand.

pleasure. After all, if billions of dollars is what some entrepreneur gets for doing a "mitzvah" he doesn't even have to do, without having had any intention to do it, then what kind of reward must a mitzvah like a halachic washing of the hands net someone if the person is commanded to do it, and has the conscious intention to do that mitzvah?

Exactly. So if you have difficulty relating to hundreds of billions of dollar as recompense for a mitzvah because it seems SO disproportionate, don't worry, it IS. A single mitzvah is worth a LOT more than billions of dollars, and all the money in the world! In fact, this is what the rabbis are telling us when they say:

> One hour of pleasure in the World-to-Come is better than all the time in this world. (Pirkei Avos 4:16)

ALL THE TIME in this world is worth a lot more than even TRILLIONS of dollars. The United States has only been in business for a few hundred years, and already the national debt is up to $21,836,687,236, 972. Man has been around for a lot longer. And yet, even just ONE HOUR of Olam HaBa is greater than all this!

Remember that $5,000,000 you got for helping the stranger get the groceries to her car? It's not even "peanuts" compared to the reward that people will receive for even a small fraction of the mitzvos they will have done throughout their lifetime. Is that not enough of an incentive to just drop everything foolish and rack up eternal merit points?

Unfortunately not.

The question is how we can change that. We are overlooking one of the most important opportunities we will ever get in life. Is it something only righteous people can take advantage of, or can others do so as well? The next chapter will answer that question.

JUST AS PEOPLE die, so do events. At the time events occur, they can be so full of life that it seems almost as if they have their own body and soul. But as they "age," their "soul" wanes until, like people who have died, they too become only a passing memory. When the events happened, thousands of words may not have been enough to describe them. Centuries later, even one sentence suffices.

A good example of this is "Mattan Torah," the "Giving of Torah." This was the most AWESOME event experienced by human beings, at least since leaving the Garden of Eden. Not only did God speak to humans, but He did so to THREE MIL-

LION men, women, and children at the SAME TIME. Mind-blowing, or at least it should be.

The Torah itself sums up the entire out-of-this-world event in a few verses, and then moves on, casually and naturally. The reader does so as well. And although we have Shavuos to remind us about what happened on that historic day, this holiday is probably the least exciting of the three chagim.[1] Why?

APPRECIATION is the key, but it unfortunately does not come at all naturally—only after GREAT effort. All the good things in life we're here to accomplish can only be the result of mesiras-Nefesh—self-sacrifice, as it says:

> According to the suffering is the reward. (Pirkei Avos 5:23)

When we appreciate something, we give it soul. When we appreciate something that was taken for granted, we resurrect both it and our connection to it. That can only ENHANCE the quality of our life, making it more exciting.

Clearly appreciation is a soul thing. The body craves excitement, feels entitled to it, but rarely appreciates the source of it. Excitement is the goal.

---

[1] The other two are Pesach and Succos.

Everyone and everything else are just the means by which to get it.

The soul has no expectations. It knows that everything in life is a gift from God, and that appreciation is necessary to fully enjoy what it gets. The more soul-oriented we are, the more appreciative of life and others we will be. Life will be richer in the ULTIMATE sense.

Here's another point about the giving of Torah that many take for granted. When God spoke to the Jewish nation at Mt. Sinai, they became completely UNIFIED, "like a single person with a single heart."[2] For a short period of time in history, all the people there put aside their differences and became unified in a way that won't happen again until Yemos HaMoshiach—the Messianic Era.

This may not sound like a big deal, but it was HUGE. The unity was messianic, which is why it will take Moshiach to achieve it again. It's one thing for a choirmaster to synchronize 150 singers, but it is something completely different to sync three MILLION people! How was it POSSIBLE?

Well, if you are God, you can do anything. God could have just zapped them and made them into zombies, and then told them what to say. But

---

[2] Rashi, Shemos 19:2.

there would have been no "fun" in that for God, Who always prefers that we do the right thing of our OWN volition. If so, then how DID God get 3,000,000 people on the same page to receive His Torah?

The answer to this question requires a short digression. We need to discuss something that scientists and psychologists are calling the hard problem of consciousness. They're calling it the "hard problem" because among all the questions science has tried to answer, the one about human consciousness is one of the most elusive. And it will continue to be, if they refuse to look for it beyond the physical realm. If they're going to limit their search for consciousness to the physical, then they might as well call it the "impossible problem."

What they have come up with so far?

Over the past decade scientists have developed what they are calling a "resonance theory of consciousness." It "suggests" that resonance, or synchronized vibrations, is the basis of human consciousness.

What does this actually mean? For starters, everything in the physical universe is continuously in motion, constantly vibrating. Even objects that APPEAR to be stationary are in fact vibrating, oscillating, and resonating at various frequencies.

All matter consists of vibrations of various underlying fields.

What is REALLY interesting is that when different vibrating objects approach one another, they will often, after some time, start to vibrate together at the same frequency and "sync." This is why, for example, we always see the same face of the moon—the moon's rotation is exactly synced with its orbit around the earth.

Synchronicity is crucial in the brain as well. In the brain electrical patterns, specifically, gamma, theta, and beta waves,[3] work together to produce what scientists call various types of human consciousness. Theta and beta waves are significantly slower than gamma waves, but the three work together to produce or at least facilitate various types of human consciousness.

Synchronization, which in this case refers to shared electrical oscillation rates, allows for smooth communication between neurons and groups of neurons. Without such synchronization, inputs would arrive at random phases of the neuron excitability cycle and would be ineffective, or

---

[3] The names refer to the speed of electrical oscillations in the various brain regions. Gamma waves are typically defined as about 30 to 90 cycles per second (hertz), theta as a 4 to 7 hz rhythm, and beta as 12.5 to 30 hz.

at least much less effective, in communication.[4]

The bottom line is that the physical world is all about VIBRATIONS. Most important of all, it is about SHARED vibrations, and THAT is the take-away point necessary to answer the original question about the messianic unity achieved at Mt. Sinai.

"Shalom bayis," literally "peace in the home," applies on many levels. It is the universal goal of life, whether between spouses, friends, or internally. It's about being on the same page as others, being in sync with them, as each Jew was with his or her fellow Jews when God gave His Torah.

The event of the giving of Torah was like a divine tuning fork that harmonized the entire Jewish nation. At Mt. Sinai, all Jews shared a common frequency and resonated together. This is what had the power to transform them into "a single person with a single heart."

But here's the part that scientists don't know, and WON'T know until they accept the reality of the spiritual world. All of THAT was not to CREATE human consciousness but rather to facilitate it, to make it possible for the source of conscious-

---

[4]"The Hippies Were Right: It's All about Vibrations, Man! (December 5, 2018) from the magazine "Scientific American."

ness—the soul—to connect to the Source of consciousness, God Himself,[5] by means of the body.

Although this sounds simple enough, there is a fundamental problem. The body and the soul belong to two entirely different realms of existence. The body is completely physical, and the soul is completely spiritual. How is it possible for them to come together? What is the common denominator that allows them to coexist?

Energy! It's the one thing in Creation that can step back and forth across the line between "Ayin" and "Yaish,"[6] the spiritual and physical worlds. Although it FUNCTIONS in the physical world, its source is in the spiritual one, which is also why scientists have a difficult time understanding what it is, even though they know how it works.

A soul, being a "spark" of the light of God, is PURE energy. Physical atoms, quantum physicists explain, are made up of vortices of energy that are constantly spinning and vibrating, each one radiating its own unique energy signature. This

---

[5] The body can't be the source of consciousness any more than a car can be its own driver, unless previously programmed by man.

[6] "Yaish" means "something," and is therefore used to refer to the physical world. "Ayin" means "nothing," and refers to the spiritual world because, compared to the physical world, it is as if it does not exist. Hence "Creation Ex Nihilo" is "Yaish m'Ayin"—"Something from Nothing."

results in a "zone" that can be shared by both the physical AND the spiritual, the body AND the soul.

Communication between the two requires that body and soul share a similar energy signature. When that frequency is disrupted, it results in death, partial or complete, depending upon the extent of the disruption.

The "good life" is not the result of material success as many think. It is the result of synchronizing body and soul. When we do this, we achieve the one thing many people seek but never really achieve: peace of mind.

This is basically what Torah does. It provides the means to sync the body with the soul, to put them on the same frequency. Hence it says about Torah:

> Its ways are ways of pleasantness, and all its paths are peace. (Mishlei 3:17)

This is also the reason there is such an emphasis on marrying one's soulmate. Why? What difference does it make? Either way you will be marrying a person who was once a total stranger.

A total stranger yes, but one who will "resonate" with us. It's not about "good chemistry" but about physics, SPIRITUAL physics. Each soul has its own unique "frequency," based upon its origin in the spiritual realm. If souls originate from the same vicinity, they will more readily sync with one another. If they don't, shalom bayis will be missing.

The Talmud warns about this:

Rebi Akiva elucidated: When a husband and wife are worthy, the Shechinah will be between them. When they are not worthy, fire consumes them. (Sotah 17a)

There is a logical explanation for this. The Hebrew word for "man" is "ish," spelled Aleph-Yud-Shin. For "woman" the Hebrew word is "ishah," spelled Aleph-Shin-Heh. The letters shared by both are Aleph and Shin, which spell "aish," or "fire." The letters unique to each are the Yud in "ish" and the Heh in "ishah." Combined, they spell a name of God.

Therefore, Rebi Akiva warned, if the Yud-Heh —the connection to God through Torah—is missing from a union of man and woman, what will remain is the word "aish," twice. Without Torah to "sync" the couple, they will end up divorced.

How does Torah sync people?

The body is inherently instinctual, selfish, a low-level frequency. The soul is godly, and therefore the highest level of frequency possible in a created entity. Through the learning of Torah and the performance of mitzvos, the body is spiritualized, increasing its frequency until it sufficiently matches that of the soul to result in a level of synchronicity.

This not only results in shalom bayis, but if the energy signature of the soul is that of God's, then by definition it also results in Olam HaBa. Therefore, when the frequency of the body approaches that of the soul, the person can access the reality of Olam HaBa through the soul. That is how and when it becomes clear to a person that all the pleasures of THIS WORLD can never match even ONE HOUR of ETERNAL PLEASURE.

This is how Shabbos can be one-sixtieth of Olam HaBa.[7] The more we tune ourself to the frequency of Shabbos, which means having the body live on the level of Shabbos, the more we are able to access, via our soul, the reality of Olam HaBa in the here and now. And if we manage to take some of the light of Shabbos into our week, we can maintain that advantage even on non-Shabbos days.[8]

---

[7] Brochos 57b.

[8] This is the reason for tradition of lighting two Shabbos candles, which represent the concept of shalom bayis, on Motzei Shabbos.

The challenge to all this is the "frequency disrupters." They're the people or events, planned or "accidental," which can unsync a person with God. Amalek and his like are chief among them, which is why God made Amalek His PERSONAL enemy.[9] Frequency disrupters are extremely invasive and all-pervasive.[10]

War, for example, is a HUGE frequency disrupter. But so is an antagonistic remark, which has the ability to upset a person and set in motion a terrible disagreement. And certainly all those things that are DESIGNED to pull the body in the direction of the non-spiritual are the greatest frequency disrupters of all, and "weapons" of Amalek.

But they deserve a chapter of their own.

---

[9] Shemos 17:16.

[10] A cell phone going off during Shemonah Esrai, even for a minute, or making a subtle "bing" to announce the arrival of a text or email, may seem like no big deal. But it is. Unlike many mechanized devices which can quickly recover their signal and pick up where they left off, people who work hard to focus on God may finish tefillah without recovering at all. It's hard enough to build kavanah without having to rebuild it.

THE JEWISH PEOPLE have had no shortage of enemies. They have made them just about everywhere they have gone. Sometimes it is their own fault, but most of the time it is just the way history works:

It is a law that Eisav hates Ya'akov. (Sifri, Be-Ha'alosecha 69)

The most horrendous of all Jewish enemies, however, is Amalek.[1] This word originally referred to the nomadic people who travelled a great dis-

---

[1] Shemos 17:8.

tance just to attack the Jewish people on their way to freedom. Their anti-Semitism was the most extreme. Whereas other anti-Semites have been satisfied just to make Jews PHYSICALLY suffer, Amalek wanted to get at their SOUL as well.

That's why God took this attack personally, vowing to be at war with Amalek "in every generation."[2] Afflicting the soul of a Jew is an attack against God, because it destroys the possibility of his or her relationship with God.

The good news is that Amalek ceased to be a people back in Sancheriv's time.[3] The bad news is that Amalek, it turns out, is more than just a people. Amalek is a CONCEPT that preceded and has lived on past the nation that first embodied it.[4]

What did Amalek do that was REALLY so bad? Nations before and after Amalek have tortured the Jewish people. Nations before and after Amalek have tried to strip Jews of their Torah identity. What was unique about Amalek that made him so reviled by God?

This is how the Torah puts it and how Rashi explains it:

---

[2] Shemos 17:16.
[3] Brochos 28a.
[4] Zohar, Ki Seitzei 281b.

Remember what Amalek did to you on the way, when you went out of Egypt, how he happened upon you on the way and cut off all the stragglers at your rear, when you were faint and weary, and he did not fear God. (Devarim 25:17-18)

It is language of cold and heat, as if to say that he made you cold and lukewarm after you had been boiling. All the nations had been afraid to go to war against you until he came and led the way. You were like a boiling hot bath into which no one could enter, until a wild person came and jumped in, scalding himself but cooling it for others. (Rashi, Devarim 25:17)

As Rashi explains, Amalek was the "first."[5] The FIRST to do WHAT? Attack the Jewish people? He was neither the first nor the last. Yes, the first to attack them after they left Egypt. But what was so uniquely bad that he was singled out more than any other anti-Semite throughout thousands of years of anti-Semitic history?

Rashi answers the question with the words, "[He was] cooling it for others." At first it sounds as

---

[5] Bamidbar 24:20.

if Amalek merely opened the door for others to attack the Jewish people because he did it first. He "cooled" off the Jewish people in the EYES OF OTHERS, by making them seem less invincible.

But didn't Amalek get clobbered? Didn't he earn the wrath of God FOREVER? Even if another nation could find a way to avoid the former, how could it be so sure that it would also avoid the latter? It's not pleasant being at war with God, especially for all of history.

The "cooling down" was rather OF the Jewish people, LITERALLY. Yes, the attack impacted the Jewish people's level of confidence, but they also saw how God fought on their behalf. Yes, they saw how stragglers were killed by Amalek, but it was a vulnerability they knew had been created by the stragglers themselves. They had caused themselves to be rejected from the protection of the Clouds of Glory. So what was "cooled down"?

To answer that question, you have to first know that the exodus from Egypt was not simply about the rescuing of a downtrodden slave nation. There have been many slave nations that God has NOT redeemed, at least not in the same spectacular way He did for the Jewish people. Redemption from Egypt was just a means to this purpose:

I am God; I called you for righteousness and I

will strengthen your hand; and I formed you, and I made you for a people's covenant, for a light unto nations. (Yeshayahu 42:6)

Until Avraham, no one had really been on the same page as God. Having figured out life, Avraham built himself into a follower of God, someone who saw life as God saw it. That earned him the right to hear directly from God, and to form an eternal covenant, the "Bris Ben HaBesarim."[6]

Avraham then passed on what he had learned and accomplished to Yitzchak, who later taught it all to Ya'akov Avinu. But it is one thing to pass on an awesome spiritual legacy from father to son, and something altogether different to build a nation of three million people from the legacy.

This could only be the result of a very long and complicated process. It began with Yosef and his brothers, and all they went through. Then it was intensified through centuries of life in Egypt, especially the slavery. And just before they left Egypt, four-fifths of the population was "filtered" out during the plague of darkness.[7]

---

6 Bereishis 15:1.

7 Rashi, Shemos 13:8. They didn't want to leave Egypt with Moshe and the nation.

This is why the ten plagues were necessary. God could easily have freed the Jewish people through natural means, like an epidemic. But He specifically sent ten plagues to expedite the spiritual development process,[8] which meant resuscitating the Aleph of each Jew who would actually leave Egypt.

The ALEPH?

WHICH Aleph?

The Aleph missing from the word "kisay" in Parashas Beshallach, for starters:

> There is a hand on the throne—kisay—of the Eternal—Yud-Heh, [that there shall be] a war for God against Amalek from generation to generation. (Shemos 17:16)

> Why is "throne" written Chof-Samech and not Chof-Samech-ALEPH?…The Holy One, Blessed is He, swore that His…throne will not be complete until the name of Amalek is completely obliterated. (Rashi)

The word should be "kisay," but without the Aleph it reads "kase," and delivers a profound message: the existence of Amalek disrupts heaven

---

[8] Drushei Olam HaTohu, Chelek, Drush 5, Anaf 4, Siman 6.

as well as earth.

Then there is the Aleph that is almost missing from the first word, "vayikra," of Sefer Vayikra. In a Sefer Torah it is written smaller than the other letters and is also raised, so that the word "vayikra" looks more like "vayi-kar," which, as Rashi explains, has the opposite meaning:

> ["Vayikra"] is an expression of love, used by the ministering angels, as it says, "One called to the other" (Yeshayahu 6:3). However, to the gentile prophets [God] revealed Himself with an expression of happenstance and uncleanness, as it says, "God chanced—VAYI-KAR—upon Bilaam" (Bamidbar 23:4, 16). (Rashi, Vayikra 1:1)

Again, the Aleph is used to communicate an important message. Its inclusion means closeness to God. Its absence means a godless relationship.

Why the Aleph, though? First of all, as mentioned earlier,[9] an Aleph is comprised of three letters, two Yuds and a Vav. Together, the three letters have a combined gematria of 26,[10] the numerical

---

[9] Chapter 7.
[10] Yud-Vav-Yud is 10+6+10 = 26

value of God's four-letter and holiest name.[11] Secondly, the numerical value of Aleph is one, and it alludes to God's oneness.

This is why Aleph is part of the name of the first man, "Adam," spelled Aleph-Dalet-Mem. Whereas the Dalet-Mem, which spells "blood," alludes to man's PHYSICAL body, the Aleph, which is a divine spark, hints to the soul component of man.

Thus the first of the ten plagues in Egypt was of blood. It was a wake-up call to the Jewish people, telling them that centuries of Egyptian exile had brought them down to the 49th level of spiritual impurity, to the level of Dalet-Mem, without the Aleph. It was time to begin the process of restoring it.

This is what the plagues did, each successive one being more miraculous and therefore more godly than the previous one. By the time God Himself carried out the tenth plague, all their Alephs had become so powerful that even free will had, at least temporarily, been suspended.[12]

This is why, as the remaining Jewish people sat down to make their first Pesach Seder, they ate

---

[11] Called the "Tetragrammaton," it is not pronounced at this time as it is written because of its tremendous holiness.
[12] Drushei Olam HaTohu, Chelek 2, Drush 5, Anaf 2, Siman 4.

matzah. It may have been the "bread of affliction," but more accurately it was the "bread of Yud," of Olam HaBa.[13] That was the level they had achieved the night just prior to leaving Egypt.

Redemption from Egypt was never about strengthening the bodies of the Jewish people. It was about strengthening their souls, about "tuning" them to the God frequency. Mitzrayim had been a hedonistic society, and just living there empowered the body over soul. Leaving Egypt, first spiritually and then physically, reversed the process.

Redemption in the ultimate sense is the automatic result of becoming a true "Adam," becoming the right combination of body and soul. Even the words themselves make this point, because the gematria of "Adam" and "geulah"—redemption—are the same.[14]

This is why, if Amalek is going to attack anything in a person, it's going to be the Aleph, the soul. Thus the Aleph of "kisay" is missing in order to indicate that as long as Amalek remains in some form, an Aleph is not safe. At the very least it will be in danger of reduction, as the small Aleph of "Vayikra" warns.

---

[13] Maharal, Haggadah Shel Pesach. See the previous chapter.
[14] "Adam" is 1+4+40 = 45, and "geulah" is 3+1+6+30+5 = 45.

THIS is why Amalek was singled out as the greatest nemesis of the Jewish people, and enemy of God. He attacks the Aleph and disrupts the frequency of the soul. He did it in Refidim,[15] and he has done it all throughout history, making a close relationship with God difficult for most, impossible for others.

Thus even after defeating Amalek and arriving at Mt. Sinai, the Jewish people were not ready for the incredible experience of hearing God. Each time God spoke, their neshamas left them temporarily,[16] and their fear of that happening again caused them to ask Moshe Rabbeinu to receive the rest of Torah on their behalf.

Becoming like a "single person with a single heart" was an amazing accomplishment, but it wasn't enough for them to become the people they were taken out of Egypt to become. We may have won the battle against Amalek at Refidim, but we had yet to win the war.

This is why only 40 days after hearing God speak, the Erev Rav[17] were able to build a golden calf and reintroduce some Egyptian hedonism

---

[15] The place at which Amalek attacked the Jewish people.

[16] Shemos Rabbah 29:3.

[17] Egyptian mixed multitude which Moshe Rabbeinu had converted and brought out of Egypt with the Jewish people.

back into the Jewish people.[18] The Aleph—not yet being strong enough to fight back—was overwhelmed, and it succumbed to the Dalet-Mem.

The result was more than catastrophic. The tablets that God had carved out, and on which He had written the Ten Commandments, were broken—Moshe Rabbeinu's response to the horrible sin of the calf. He then punished its perpetrators.

After 40 days of praying for forgiveness, God had Moshe Rabbeinu replace the broken tablets. But these were tablets that Moshe himself had carved out, not God, on which He rewrote the Ten Commandments. Spiritually, they were not at all the same.

Kabbalah explains that the first tablets were messianic. They did not talk about laws to do with the permissible and forbidden, the pure and impure, etc., as our version of Torah does. They spoke about messianic life, the resurrection of the dead, and Olam HaBa. That was THEIR level of reality.[19]

---

[18] Shemos 32:1.

[19] If only the Jewish people had merited the Torah that had been given to them, the Luchos HaRishonos—First Tablets… which is the Torah of the future, the Torah of Atzilus, the sod of the Aitz HaChaim…They were an awesome unity from the top to the bottom, and had we merited them, they would have brought about the tikun of unity below and eliminated all the impurity (Drushei Olam HaTohu, Chelek 2, Siman 12, Ch. 1, Os 3).

Receiving the first tablets would have meant ending history then, and beginning the Messianic Era at that time. All the bad history since then would not have occurred, including the destruction of the First Temple.[20] History would have been entirely different, MESSIANIC, for which we are still waiting.

And wait we will, because the door Amalek opened is not an easy one to close. The interference pattern he created reverberates to this very day, perhaps even more so in these final generations. It has left us a nation spiritually vulnerable, and in danger of attack from an enemy that, for all intents and purposes, is as bad if not worse than Amalek himself.

---

[20] The Luchos Shnios—Second Tablets—were given to them, which is Toras Beriyah, the sod of the Aitz HaDa'as Tov v'Ra. The Gevuros within them are the negative mitzvos, which are to protect a person and distance him from evil and impurity...They cannot rectify the world at all, only those people who learn them and adhere to them, which enables the people to ascend and become unified with the light of the Luchos HaRishonos, and taste from the radiance of the Aitz HaChaim (Drushei Olam HaTohu, Chelek 2, Siman 12, Ch. 1, Os 3).

chapter eleven *core beliefs*

THE ARIZAL SAYS that the Erev Rav, the "mixed multitude," consisted of actual converts. He explains that they had been a community of Egyptians who felt more akin to Ya'akov's family than to their fellow Egyptians, and gravitated towards them over the years. By the time they left Egypt with Moshe Rabbeinu, they numbered 6,000,000.[1]

Others say that the Erev Rav were rabble-rousers, sent along by Pharaoh to act as spies.[2] Even though God had decimated Egypt with 10

---

[1] Sha'ar HaPesukim, Parashas Shemos.
[2] Orach HaChaim, Shemos 13:7.

plagues, Pharaoh only agreed to let the Jewish people take a three-day leave of absence. The Erev Rav was sent along to make sure his slave nation came back to continue serving him.

In the end, it really doesn't make much of a difference, because in any case the Erev Rav succeeded in disrupting the Jewish mission. What started with the disaster of the golden calf at Mt. Sinai would end with the most dangerous war the Jewish people ever fought, a do-or-die war.[3]

The Zohar enumerates five categories of Erev Rav:

> Nefilim, Giborim, Anakim, Repha'im, and Amalekim… (Zohar, Bereishis 25a)

The Vilna Gaon explained how they are identified:

> The five types of Erev Rav are (1) those who create strife and speak loshon hara; (2) those who pursue their desires, etc.; (3) the cheats who pretend to be righteous but whose hearts are not straight; (4) those who pursue honor and build great synagogues to make a name for themselves; (5) those who pursue money and strife. (Aderes Eliyahu)

---

[3] Kol HaTor, Ch. 2:2:2.

But there's a problem. Is it really so black and white? Are these criteria enough to single out individuals or groups, call them "Erev Rav," and then declare war against them? Many a "ba'al teshuvah"[4] may have once fit into one or more of these categories, and many religious people still do. Are they automatically Erev Rav?

What if we're WRONG?

What if we're ONE of them?

It's very hard to fight an existential war against enemies you can only vaguely identify, especially if, as the GR"A says, they work by trickery and sleight of hand. Today's friend might be tomorrow's backstabber, while a perceived enemy might in fact be a true ally. Is God the only One Who can truly fight this war?

Classically, yes AND no.

The Talmud states that without God's help, we cannot possibly overcome the challenges of the yetzer hara,[5] and that ultimately every battle finds its way to the yetzer hara. No matter which enemy we fight on the outside, the main battle is the one with the "enemy" on the inside, and THAT does require the help of God.

But God's help comes in many forms and

---

4 Someone who returns to a Torah lifestyle.
5 Kiddushin 30b.

sizes. It might be an outright miracle or one that comes from people exhibiting more mettle than they thought they had. Either way, divine help is predicated on something that only WE can build, and that's our CORE BELIEFS and VALUES.

Core values are the fundamental beliefs regarding what is right and wrong in life. As a result, these dictate our behavior and help us determine our path through life. For the most part, they are what society hands down from one generation to the next, but each one of us, by virtue of our intelligence and free will, must ratify them for ourself.

One could develop an accurate set of core beliefs just from life itself, as Avraham Avinu did. But most people either do not care or know how to, so they just stick with what they have been bequeathed by society and picked up from life's experiences.

This is why God gave Torah. It is GOD'S set of core beliefs, at least for mankind. We are supposed to learn these, compare them to our current core beliefs, and then replace those we got wrong with the right ones. That is the basis of "teshuvah" or "repentance."

And as we do this, replacing our false assumptions about life with true ones, our perception of life will automatically become adjusted. Perceptions are based upon assumptions; the truer the assumptions, the truer the perception, and this will in turn affect our actions.

This is where we make our last stand, so to speak. Our core beliefs define us and our life. Ignoring them is a form of suicide. Core beliefs are what make life meaningful, and the more meaningful our core beliefs are, the more meaningful our life will be.

At the end of the day, and of history for that matter, it is on the battlefield of core beliefs that the final war will take place. War is always a function of one nation's core beliefs against another's, but the FINAL war, the war of ALL wars, will be the world's core beliefs against God's. THAT is the War of Gog and Magog:

> It is taught: Gerrim Gerurim...when they see the War of Gog and Magog, [they] will say to [Gog and Magog], "Why have you come?"
>
> They will answer, "[To fight] against God and His Moshiach." (Avodah Zarah 3b)

That's why the War of Gog and Magog will take place, to test a person's core beliefs. Many people go through life untested, but since the War of Gog and Magog is the threshold to the Messianic Era, which is by invitation only, EVERYONE'S core beliefs will have to be tested. Survival will not come down to PHYSICAL weaponry, but rather SPIRITUAL weaponry—it will come down to CORE BELIEFS and VALUES.

That is how the War of Gog and Magog can be mitigated. The more the proponents of the final war match God's core-belief system, the less of a war the physical one will have to be. The less they match God's, the greater the physical war will be, as described by the prophets Yeshayahu, Yechezkel, and Zechariah. Negative prophecies don't have to be fulfilled, but if the world doesn't get its act together soon, they will be.

It is important that our core beliefs enable us to ensure that we are not part of the Erev Rav, and that we can fight against joining them. The people who lead the war against Torah values might clearly be Erev Rav, even if they are religious. But because of how they carefully couch their activities in idealistic goals, they can drag many after them, people whose core beliefs would not really match those of the Erev Rav if they knew better.

The truth usually comes out at some time, but "better late than never" is not always good enough. Sometimes late can be almost as bad as never, because irreversible damage might have occurred. At some point people may regret their actions, but if they have already gone past the point of no return, they will be forced to live with the consequences.

The Talmud tells us that we should do teshuvah one day before we die.[6] But how can we know the day of our death before it happens? Therefore the Talmud says that we should do teshuvah EVERY DAY—whether we are young or old—in case it is our last one.

What does that mean? It means taking the time to find out what our core beliefs are, and whether or not they are ultimately true. It means checking out where they came from, and the reliability of the source. It means not being afraid to change them if it turns out that they are false, even if doing so is very uncomfortable, and then acting accordingly.

This is why the Vilna Gaon says that in the final war against the Erev Rav we either fight against them or we are on their side. There is no neutral position in this war. And he concludes that if we are not against the Erev Rav, we would have been better off not being born at all!

Those are very strong words. But if the point of life is to develop true core beliefs and values, and then live by them, then a person who hasn't done so is not really living. It is as if he weren't even born, in a matter of speaking—in GOD'S

---

[6] Shabbos 153a.

manner of speaking.

So what ARE the Torah's CORE BELIEFS? The Rambam answered this question with his "13 Principles of Faith," printed in most siddurim:

1. Belief in the existence of the Creator, who is perfect in every manner of existence and is the Primary Cause of all that exists.
2. The belief in God's absolute and unparalleled unity.
3. The belief in God's non-corporeality and that He will never be affected by any physical occurrences, such as movement, rest, or dwelling.
4. The belief in God's eternity.
5. The imperative to worship God exclusively and no foreign false gods.
6. The belief that God communicates with man through prophecy.
7. The belief in the primacy of the prophecy of Moshe our teacher.
8. The belief in the divine origin of the Torah.
9. The belief in the immutability of the Torah.
10. The belief in God's omniscience and providence.
11. The belief in divine reward and retribution.
12. The belief in the arrival of the Moshi-

ach and the Messianic Era.

13. The belief in the resurrection of the dead.

Although these 13 principles may sound like just a bunch of religious tenets, they address every possible aspect of life. Each principle taken to heart impacts the way we approach each moment of daily life. Each principle "tunes" us to the frequency of God, so that we resonate with His energy.

You can't believe in these principles and be part of the Erev Rav. You can't believe in these principles and be influenced by the Erev Rav either. You don't HAVE to know who is part of the Erev Rav and who isn't. By learning these principles and taking them to heart, you go to war against the Erev Rav, WHOEVER you are, WHEREVER you are.

The Erev Rav's desire is to turn everyone to their way of thinking, expressed by the following words:

"These are your gods, Israel, which brought you up out of Egypt!" (Shemos 32:4)

It would be a mistake to just dismiss these words as religious rhetoric with no application in modern times. They apply today just as much as they ever have, and perhaps even more so. You just have to understand what they mean in order to understand their current relevance, how licentiousness today is as much a result of these words as it was back at the base of Mt. Sinai.

What did the Erev Rav mean by these words? The Jewish people weren't born yesterday. They knew which God had taken them out of Egypt. Were the Erev Rav so naive as to think that the Jewish people would accept that a golden calf had pulled off the ten plagues and engineered their escape from what had been the mightiest nation on earth at that time?

Of course not. That would be trying to appeal to their seichel, their minds. The Erev Rav were far too wily for that. Instead, they did what they do best. They bypassed the seichel and went right for the heart. They weren't telling the Jewish people, or at least the elements that would listen to them, that they owed allegiance to the calf. They were showing them that they COULD if they wanted to.

What does THAT mean?

Anyone who thinks that the world is divided between the religious and non-religious is wrong. EVERYONE is religious. The only real difference between people is to what they pledge their allegiance. Man is inherently a worshipper of something, but it is up to him to decide of what.

God-worshippers may get up early to serve Him, but businessmen who "worship" the dollar may also get up early. Those who serve God may follow strict rules, but so do athletes who "serve" the god of victory. People pray to the God of Creation while secular people make requests for the things they need from those more "powerful" than they are. That's just the way we are.

But whereas some will only worship the true God, others prefer to worship gods they themselves have empowered. They imbue things with supernatural powers to make them seem godly, while being far less demanding than God Himself. In the case of the golden calf, for example, they made a god who even supports hedonism.

This is a classic case of having your cake and eating it too. You can have a sense of religion, but without religious obligations. You can believe in something greater than you, while being able to act as if it were really lesser. It's actually self-worship, deflected to a made-up deity so that it is not so obviously silly.

And dangerous. As the Torah states, "God is a jealous God," which means that He has zero tolerance for idol worship, be it Jewish or gentile. He may put up with it for a while because of the rules of free will, but as the Erev Rav learned at Mt. Sinai, the boom, one way or another, will eventually come down on the perpetrators.

It was a lot easier in pagan times to sell such a bag of hot air. People were incredibly ignorant, and fear ran their lives. At the same time, people could be very greedy and hedonistic, and this combination made for some very "interesting" religions in the early days.

Man has since become a lot smarter and far more sophisticated, but not actually very different. He has the same desires today as he has always had, the same need to worship something while at the same time not obligating himself in ways that are secularly uncomfortable.

Therefore the Erev Rav has had to devise modern methods to accomplish the same thing it has always done: hold the door open for those looking to escape God. And as the Vilna Gaon points out, the Erev Rav is so good at making itself look righteous that even people who mean well often fall for it, and get destroyed along the way.

The only defense is proper core beliefs. If these align with Torah, we will not only be protected, but we can even expect divine help to remain that way. This is what the Talmud ultimately means when it says, "All is in the hands of Heaven except for the fear of Heaven."[7]

---

[7] Brochos 33b.

This does not mean fear in the conventional sense, but more in the sense of "seeing" a fear that comes from having learned what the world looks like from God's perspective. That is what defines us and gives us the ability to know when a certain philosophy is really the truth, and when it is only masquerading as truth.

ONE OF THE most famous lines in English literature is "To thine own self be true."[1] Although it seems easy enough to explain, many interpretations of these words have been offered over the ages since they were first said.

The question is, however, how it's possible to be true to your TRUE self if you don't know what it is. One person may think he is being true to himself when he looks out only for his own interests. Another person may think he is being true to his self when he lets his inner convictions, right or wrong, rule over those of others.

---

[1] Hamlet, Act 1, Scene 3.

The confusion often vanishes when the word "self" is replaced with the word "soul," so that the statement becomes "To thine own SOUL be true." Souls are not selfish. Souls are about only inner convictions that are truthful and ultimately meaningful. If we are true to our SOUL, our time on earth will be highly productive, and in Olam HaBa it will be highly rewarded.

There is another level to this as well. It has to do with something called "soul nature." No two souls are exactly the same, even in identical twins, and many souls are VERY different from one another. There is NOTHING a person can do about THAT.

Physically there ARE things we can change about ourselves. DNA engineering can alter physical features before a child is even born. We can wear shoes to make us taller, color our hair to make it look different, lose weight to become thinner. Plastic surgery can completely change a person's appearance.

Not so with a soul. It can be rectified and improved, but never changed. Its nature will always be inherent to its existence, which is why, as hard as we may try to change our spiritual essence, we can't. Souls that are prone to anger will ALWAYS be prone to anger, and those for whom chesed comes easily will ALWAYS be that way.

This might sound unfair or, in the language of the Greeks, tragic, if not for the fact that we are never responsible for how we were created, but only for what we do after we were created. "According to the effort is the reward"[2] applies to all of us equally, which means that we're not graded on our "givens" but rather on how we use them.

So if someone has a soul nature that makes it easy to become frustrated, and he feels like blowing up at the people who have made him feel that way but doesn't, he is a hero in God's eyes. If he only gets partially angry because he holds back the rest of his anger, he is still a hero in God's eyes because it takes a LOT of WILLPOWER to do that, and that's what God made the world for.

Likewise, a person who is naturally patient does not get very much reward for being that way. He may make lots of friends and get promoted quickly, but from Heaven's point of view, he hasn't really accomplished that much since it does not require much WILL for him to be that way. He has to find something else that he has to work at in order to excel.

There's no sense trying to be something that our soul just isn't. We can be envious of birds, which naturally fly, but we accepted our inability

---

2 Pirkei Avos 5:23.

to fly the same way as birds and worked to find another way to accomplish the same thing. Now we too can fly south for the winter—we just need a boarding pass to do it.

It may be simple to figure out what we need to rectify but challenging to actually effect it. We will not only need to know the difference between right and wrong, but also what to do with this knowledge. For example, losing one's temper is not acceptable in Judaism, but for some people, it is almost impossible to avoid in certain situations.

Likewise, it is important to be disciplined and carry out mitzvos at their right time. For some people this is never a problem, but for others it is a daily struggle just to show up on time, day after day after day.

A moment of crisis is never the right time to work on one's self. But it can be the time to reveal where the self is already holding. During a crisis too much is going on. Emotions often run high and confusion reigns. That's why people train for crises, to limit the need to come to terms with them while they are occurring.

Every mitzvah is, in fact, a crisis. It's a moment when a person has to confront reality and respond to it in a Torah way. Usually that means confronting the yetzer hara in some way, which results in conflict and crisis. And although the moment may not have seemed particularly exciting and passed rather quietly, an important battle may have been lost to the yetzer hara. Many a good person has lost his or her way during such moments.

It's all the time that we have between the crises that we are able to use to prepare for such battles. It's during the "quiet" moments that we are able to think about our core beliefs and essential nature. It's the time for a soul accounting, a "Cheshbon haNefesh" in Hebrew, to figure out how to better prepare to do the right thing when it is not the soul's nature to easily do it.

It's the difference between a "warrior" and a "worrier." It's interesting how a few letters can so dramatically change the meaning of words. A warrior is aggressive and lives with the reality of war, on some level, as a fundamental part of everyday life. He was born ready to fight.

Worriers are passive. They live in fear of worst-case scenarios and pray that they will somehow avoid or at least survive them. They're not ready for ANYTHING, believing that worrying somehow keeps them prepared and in the best defensive posture. This is not a productive and meaningful way to go through life, to say the least. It seems like the easy way out, but it's not, especially given the long-term cost.

If it sounds like a lot of work to be a "warrior," it IS. However, that's only a problem with respect to something you shouldn't have to do but are forced to do in order to accomplish some goal in life. That is not the case here at all—it actually IS the goal in life. It is life in the fullest sense. It is being a spiritual opportunist, and there is no opportunist that is more glorious than that.

This has definitely not been the way of mankind. Looking down from Above, history seems like one long ongoing pursuit of physical gratification. Even religions that have arisen over the millennia have approached spirituality in very physical ways. There will always be exceptions of course, but overall mankind has NOT been true to its soul.

The Talmud says the following:

Rebi Alexandri, on concluding his prayer, used to add the following: "Master of the Universe! It is well known to You that our will is to perform Your will. What prevents us? The 'yeast in the dough' and the subjection to foreign powers. May it be Your will to deliver us from their hand, so that we may return to perform the laws of Your will with a perfect heart!" (Brochos 17a)

The "yeast in the dough" is obviously a reference to the yetzer hara. Man was "kneaded" from the earth, so he is compared to dough. Because of the sin of the Aitz HaDa'as Tov v'Ra, the Tree of Knowledge of Good and Evil, he absorbed the yetzer hara that was once embodied only in the snake. And after it "moved in," it has acted like a "homeowner."

Since then we have had a lot more difficult time listening to our soul, which LIVES to connect to God and do the "right" thing. It is the "goody two shoes" within all of us, and its ability to steer people straight depends upon how powerful the yetzer hara is.

For most people, it has been VERY powerful, apparently, resulting in rampant assimilation over the ages and increased hester panim, the "hiding of God's face." From that point on, it's just a matter of time until the Jewish people are exiled, making the service of God even more difficult.

If one word can sum up Jewish history over the last few thousand years, it is "compromise." Exile forces Jews to constantly compromise spiritually—some more than others—but few are able to serve God under ideal conditions. It may not be hard to be a Jew, but it is certainly hard to be a true one when so much works against you in exile.

One might think that this is a statement about European Jewry over the last two millennia, and it is. But it applies equally today and, in many respects, even more so today. Exile has many forms, and although physical exile may hurt a lot more than spiritual exile, it is spiritual exile that can do the most long-term damage. Who needs God when they think they need nothing?

Thus when Rebi Alexandri speaks about "foreign powers," he does not just mean military invasion from other countries. He also means CULTURAL invasion, those who talk to the "yeast" within us, and draw us in the opposite direction from sincere and humble service of God, the true love of our soul. Anyone who is unsure of THAT should read Shir HaShirim, the "Song of Songs."

Speaking of Shlomo HaMelech (who wrote Shir HaShirim), he also had this message for all of us:

> The end of the matter, everything having been heard: fear God and keep His commandments, for this is the entire man. (Koheles 12:13)

That's right, the ENTIRE man. And that's from the mouth of a man who had it all, and then some. He wrote "Koheles" to share that with us, to save us the trouble of chasing after mere things, thinking that they lead to happiness, when in fact, as he concludes, only fear of God and His commandments do that.

Why? Because we are our souls, not our bodies, not even partially. And only by being true to our souls can we be true to ourselves, which are one and the same thing. This is the secret of life. Not because few people know about it, but rather because few people believe it. You can tell the people who do. They're the ones who have a sense of completion by simply being who they are.

What an awesome gift!

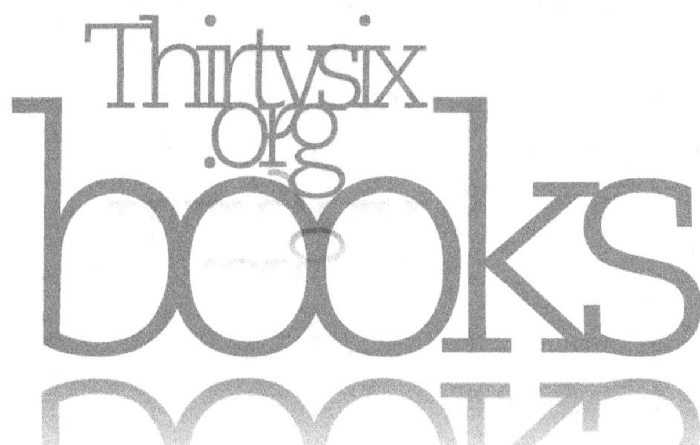

The following titles are all the books written over the years. Some books may no longer be in print, but many are still available in either PDF or Kindle formats. Visit the Thirtysix.org OnLine Bookstore, of Amazon for more information, or to order online.

Unbroken Chain of Jewish Tradition, 1985
The Eternal Link, 1990
If Only I Were Wealthy, 1992
If Only I Understood Why, 1993
If Only I Could See the Forest, 1993
If Only I Could Stay, 1993
If Only Great Was Greater, 1993
The Y Factor, 1994
Life's A Thrill, 1994
No Atheists in a Foxhole, 1994
Changes that Last Forever, 1994

The Making of a Great Jewish Leader, 1994
Bereishis: A Beginning With No End, 1994
The Wonderful World of Thirtysix, 1995
Redemption to Redemption, 1997
The Big Picture, 1998
Perceptions, 1998
Not Just Another Scenario, 2001
At The Threshold, 2001
Anticipating Redemption, 2002
Sha'ar HaGilgulim, 2002
Hadran, 2004
Talking About The End of Days, 2005
Talking About Eretz Yisroel, 2005
The Physics of Kabbalah, 2006
Be Positive, 2007
Geulah b'Rachamim, 2007
God.calm, 2007
Just Passing Through, 2007
On The Same Page, 2007
The Equation of Life, 2007
No Such Victim, 2009
Survival in 10 Easy Steps, 2009
Not Just Another Scenario 2, 2011
All In Your Mind, 2011
The Light of ThirtySix, 2011
The Last Exile, 2011
Drowning in Pshat, 2012
Drown No More, 2012

Shas Man, 2013
The Mystery of Jewish History, 2013
Survival Guide For the End-of-Days, 2013
2016, 2013
Deeper Perceptions, 2013
Chanukah Lite, 2015
The Hitchhiker's Guide to Armageddon, 2016
Purim Lite, 2016
Pesach Lite, 2016
The Torah Empowerment Seminar, 2016
Siman Tov, 2016
The Fabric of Reality, 2016
Addendum, 2016
Fundamentals of Reincarnation, 2017
Reincarnation Clarified, 2016
All About Energy, 2017
What Goes Around, 2017
The God Experience, 2017
What in Heaven, 2017
The God Experience, Part 2, 2017
The God Experience, Part 3, 2017
It's About Time, 2017
Need to Know, 2017
Perceptions, Volume 2, 2017
Once Revealed, Twice Concealed, 2017
The Art of Chayn, 2017
A Matter of Laugh or Death, 2018
Geulah b'Rachamim Program, V. 1, 2018

Geulah b'Rachamim Program, V. 2, 2018
Geulah b'Rachamim Program, V. 3, 2018
Point of Acceptance, 2018
See Ya, 2018
In Discussion: Bereishis, 2018
Reincarnation Again, 2018
A Separate Matter, 2018
In Discussion: Shemos, 2018
A Search for Self, 2019

For more information regarding any of these books or other projects, write to pinchasw@thirtysix.org, especially if you are interested in making a dedication in an upcoming publication.